PLACES WE PLAY

IRELAND'S SPORTING HERITAGE

Laytown Races, County Meath

PLACES WE PLAY

IRELAND'S SPORTING HERITAGE

Mike Cronin and Roisín Higgins

The Collins Press

First published in 2011 by
The Collins Press
West Link Park
Doughcloyne
Wilton
Cork

© Mike Cronin and Roisín Higgins

British Library Cataloguing in Publication data

Cronin, Mike.
  Places we play : Ireland's sporting heritage.
  1. Sports facilities–Ireland–History. 2. Sports–
  Ireland–History.
  I. Title II. Higgins, Roisin.
  796'.068415-dc22

ISBN-13: 9781848891296

Design & typesetting by Burns Design
Typeset in Adobe Garamond
Printed in Italy by Printer Trento

**An Roinn
Ealaíon, Oidhreachta agus Gaeltachta**
**Department of
Arts, Heritage and the Gaeltacht**

CONTENTS

Acknowledgements   vi

1 **Introduction**   1

2 **Heritage in Ireland**   9

3 **Sport and Society**   17

4 **Sport in Ireland**   29

5 **Infrastructure**   43

6 **Institutions**   59

7 **Sporting Places**   67

8 **Sporting Heritage**   81

9 **Major Sites**   89
   Aviva Stadium, Lansdowne Road, Dublin   89
   Croke Park, Dublin   93
   The Curragh, Kildare   97
   Dalymount Park, Dublin   103
   North of Ireland Cricket Club, Ormeau,
   Belfast   106
   The National Boxing Stadium, Dublin   109
   Shelbourne Park, Dublin   115
   Royal Dublin Society (RDS) Showgrounds,
   Dublin   119
   Windsor Park, Belfast   124

10 **Sport-Specific Sites**   129
   Fitzgerald Stadium, Killarney   129
   Casement Park, Belfast   133
   Cork County Cricket Club, The Mardyke,
   Cork   139
   Carlow (Rugby) Football Club, Oak Park,
   Carlow   142
   Handball Courts, Coláiste Einde, Galway   146
   Lahinch Golf Club, Clare   149
   The Markets Field, Limerick   155

   Fitzwilliam Tennis Club, Dublin   159
   Railway Union Bowls Club, Dublin   162
   Blackrock and Dun Laoghaire Baths, Dublin   164
   Belvedere Hunting Lodge, Westmeath   169
   Down Royal Racecourse, Down   173
   Garda Rowing Club, Dublin   180
   Road Bowling, Armagh and Cork   182
   Royal St George Yacht Club, Dun Laoghaire   186
   The Gordon Bennett Motor Race, Carlow,
   Kildare, Laois   190
   Pembroke Hockey Club, Dublin   193
   Ballynahinch Castle, Galway   196
   Donore Harriers, Dublin   200
   The Rás Tailteann   202
   North West 200, Antrim and Derry   209

11 **Site-Specific Heritage**   213
   Big House: Avondale, Wicklow   213
   Private School: Wilson's Hospital, Westmeath   217
   University: Trinity College Dublin   220
   Workplace: ALSAA, Dublin   226
   Private: Woodbrook Golf Club, Wicklow   228
   Multisport: Phoenix Park, Dublin   230
   Sporting Memorials   234
   Vanished: Baldoyle Races, Dublin   238
   Temporary: Laytown Races, Meath   241
   Imagined: National Stadium, Dublin, and the
   Northern Ireland Stadium, Maze Prison site,
   Down   246
   Tourism: K Club, Kildare   249
   Naming   251

Conclusion   254

Select Bibliography   257

Index   259

This book has grown out of the Irish Sporting Heritage Project, which is available to visit online at www.irishsportingheritage.com. The project is funded by the Department of Transport, Tourism and Sport and the Department of Arts, Heritage and Community and was created in order to build a record of Ireland's built sporting heritage from the 1850s onwards. We have to offer thanks to Niall Ó Donnchú and Donagh Morgan for their invaluable support throughout the lifetime of this project and their enthusiasm every time we spoke with them. Michael Kennedy co-ordinated a national audit of existing sports facilities for the Department of Arts Sport and Tourism in 2009, and we were able to build upon this valuable work. One of the great pleasures of working on this project has been the opportunity to meet people who are involved in sport in a voluntary or professional capacity. We hope this book, in some way, does justice to the commitment and energy it takes to maintain sporting clubs across the country. The big idea behind the project was in many ways borrowed from the amazing work of Simon Inglis, in his ongoing series, *Played In Britain*. Simon has always been tremendously supportive of all that we have done, and has been a mine of information. Equally important for guidance, as always, have been the faculty at the International Centre for Sports History and Culture at De Montfort University, notably Dick Holt and Dil Porter. The guidance offered by Doug Booth, and his conceptualisation of his own project on Bondi Beach, was invaluable and much appreciated. Also invaluable was the help of Kevin Baird from the Irish Heritage Trust, Peter Smyth of the Irish Sports Council and Sarah O'Connor of the Federation of Irish Sports.

The project was based in Boston College – Ireland. The people with whom we share the building make it a wonderful place to work. Thea Gilien runs the building with great panache and has always been happy to assist the project. Claire McGowan has been an invaluable addition to the Irish Sporting Heritage Project, and has cheerfully helped in many ways with all aspects of its execution. Our colleagues in the GAA Oral History Project are always happy to share information from their rich archive and we would like to thank Arlene Crampsie, Regina Fitzpatrick and Ben Shorten for their open-door policy. Paul Rouse and Mark Duncan read the manuscript and, as always, provided insightful comments. Mark has also shared his wealth of knowledge on photographic material. Eoghan, Barbara and Kerry Clear always provide good conversation and good counsel.

Colleagues in Boston provided the expertise with which to build the database for the project at www.irishsportingheritage.com. In particular we would like to acknowledge the hard work of Shelley Bame-Aldred and Sarah Castricum. At Walker Communications Callum Stewart created the website and continues to provide support. Peter Higgins has, as always, brought enthusiasm and good nature to his advice on all aspects of design. He also took some beautiful photographs and his help is really appreciated. For many of the photographs we are grateful for the work and the miles of travelling undertaken by Damien Murphy, whose other work can be viewed at www.murchu.net

For the images and information in this book we thank the various repositories and individuals who made the material available including:

Maurice Ahern (Donore Harriers), Michael Barry, Keith Beatty (Ballymoney Museum), Peter Beirne (Clare County Library), Mike Bolton (Irish Real Tennis Association), Michael Boyd (Irish Football Association), David Browne, Pat Browne (Munster Images), Gerry Byrne, William Campbell (Irish Football Association), Dan Carberry, Plunkett Carter, Brian Connolly (Johnston Central Library, Cavan), Richard T. Cooke, Patsy Costello, Nigel Daly (Railway Union Bowls), Tom Daly, Susie Dardis, Donal Donovan, Leslie Dowley, Sarah English, Louise Farrell, Brigid Geoghegan (Belvedere House), Kevin Gilligan, Jim Higgins (Galway Heritage Officer), Michael Holland (University College Cork), Tom Hunt, Nick Kelly, Seamus Kelly, Joe Kirwan (National Boxing Stadium), Shay Larkin (An Poc Fada), Anne and Seán Lynch, Bryan Lyons, Pat McCarthy, John McCullen (Superintendent, Phoenix Park), Peter McKenna (Croke Park), Peter McKitterick, Michael Maguire (Limerick City Library), Michael Molloy (Dublin City Library), John Morrison, Maria Moynihan Lee (Volvo Ocean Race, Galway), Dermot Mulligan (Carlow County Museum), Martin Mulligan (Garda Boat Club), Martin Murphy (Aviva Stadium), Liam O'Callaghan, Michael O'Doherty (Football Association of Ireland), Peter O'Doherty, Sarah O'Shea (Irish Football Association), Barbara Pratt (Wilson's Hospital), Ciarán Priestley, Dawn Quinn (Irish Greyhound Board), Peter Rigney (Irish Railway Record's Society), Mark Reynolds (GAA Museum and Archives), Paul Russell (North of Ireland Cricket Club), Áine Ryan, Ann Marie Smith, Orla Strumble (Irish Greyhound Board), Don Stewart (National Boxing Stadium).

Personally, we say thanks for the constant love and support of our families, who lived with, and visited with us, the strange world of sporting sites: from Mike, thanks and all my love to Moynagh (who helped in so many ways, showed me things I never knew existed in Ireland's sporting world, and for all her love and support), Ellen and Samson (for running around and delighting in the possibility of sport, even in their own backyard); from Roisín, thanks to Geraldine, Vincent, Peter, Claire, Rob, Paula, Maria, Liadan and Conor, the strong team at my back, and with whom I have shared many of my most important memories of Ireland's sport, its history and heritage. I am particularly grateful to my mum for bringing us up on stories of Belfast Celtic, and to the memory of my dad for all the time we spent in the Glens of Antrim.

1

INTRODUCTION

Just off St Stephen's Green in Dublin, on Earlsfort Terrace, is the National Concert Hall. This building, and those surrounding it, were the original home of University College, Dublin. The university as a whole moved to its current site at Belfield from 1964, and closed its few remaining offices at Earlsfort Terrace in 2007. Despite this, the site has not been fully redeveloped, and many buildings retain the look and feel of a university campus. One building in particular seems more overtly abandoned since its former university use. This large brick building, with a pitched glass roof, and standing directly opposite the Conrad Hotel. It is not a particularly pleasing building, and it does not seem to have, at first glance, any aesthetic or architectural value. Inside it lies largely empty, having been used by the University, at various times, as a gymnasium and a chemistry laboratory. There are various lines and markings on the floor and walls of the building, and these, along with the excellent light that pours through the glass roof, give a few clues as to why the building was constructed, and why it remains, to this day, significant to Irish heritage. This building, constructed in 1885 by Edward Guinness, was, and remains, Ireland's only covered Real Tennis court. Guinness lived at 80 St Stephen's Green, and built the court in his back garden (the remainder of which, Iveagh Gardens, was given to University College, Dublin, in 1908). The solid-looking building was constructed with a brick facade, a marble-lined interior and vaulted skylight roof in glass. The court was held in such high regard that the 1890 Real Tennis world championship was played there, and won by British-born American Tom Pettit. In 1939, Rupert Edward Cecil Lee Guinness donated the court to the nation in the expectation that the court would remain in use. Unfortunately, University College, Dublin moved in and the court was used for other purposes. After the University's departure to Belfield, the Office of Public Works eventually indicated that they would assist the Irish Real Tennis Association in restoring the building and its court to a playable state. However, at the time of writing, the renovations have still not begun.

While the setting for one of the more esoteric sports of Ireland, the fate of the Real Tennis court demonstrates the peculiar problems associated with sporting sites. While the Irish, in common with many other nationalities, have a great love of sport, the places in which games are played are infrequently viewed as being important in terms of national heritage. It is true that supporters and followers of teams often speak of 'loving' their home ground, but they also expect that the fabric of their stadium will move forward in line with contemporary trends in facility provision, comfort, and health and safety regulations. After all, no one wants to sit in a draughty stadium in a seat that is uncomfortable and where the view is restricted. For all the nostalgia and memories that circulated when the demolition of Lansdowne Road began in 2007, the high-tech Aviva Stadium has been roundly applauded for its

The real tennis court at Earlsfort Terrace was designed by the in-house architect at Guinness, Wesley William Wilson, for Edward Guinness and completed in 1885 (photo: Damien Murphy).

Right: In an age before electric light, indoor games, especially one as fast moving as real tennis, relied on huge amounts of natural light. The original glass roof of the real tennis court at Earlsfort Terrace, shown here, has survived intact (photo: Damien Murphy).

Built for a man with the wealth of Edward Guinness, the fixtures and fittings in the real tennis court were of the highest order. While much was lost or damaged over the years, as the building's usage changed, some, such as the handcrafted stair banisters speak to the building's former glory (photo: Damien Murphy).

facilities, efficiency and excellent sight lines. So long as the Irish Rugby Football Union and the Football Association of Ireland remained on Lansdowne Road (no matter what name the new stadium would be given), most supporters accepted that the building of a new stadium was necessary. For them, the issue of a sporting 'home', had more to do with place (Dublin 4), as opposed to the building itself. The Aviva is, however, different from most sporting sites around the country. Its purpose is to serve the needs of up to 50,000 paying spectators watching major rugby and soccer matches. Most sporting sites around Ireland are there for those who play rather than those who watch. Many such sites are private clubs, such as golf and tennis clubs, while others cater for team sports like Gaelic games, soccer, rugby, hockey and so on where the primary concern is players rather than large numbers of spectators.

What all sporting sites have in common, whether for players or spectators, is that they are part of the fabric of Irish history and society. Most sporting sites emerged as part of the Victorian sporting revolution, in the later decades of the nineteenth century, and most have been in a state of transformation and adaptation ever since. This book will explore the development of modern sport in Ireland, and how a built heritage was constructed for those who wished to play. In doing so, it will highlight the central place of sport in Irish social and commercial life, and explore how agencies such as the railways, the army, Churches, schools and workplaces all assisted in the development of Ireland's sporting landscape. Ireland's built sporting heritage is not, when compared to Britain or

Finished in 2010, the Aviva Stadium is one of Ireland's most contemporary sporting sites, and sits on the site of the old Lansdowne Road Stadium, which began life as a sports venue in the 1870s. Initially leased from the Pembroke Estate for a ground rent of £60 per annum, it now houses one of the most expensive structures ever built in the Irish Republic (photo: Aviva Stadium).

The Listowel and Ballybunnion Lartigue Railway was completed in 1888, and ran until 1924. It was the world's first commercial monorail. In 1893, Ballybunnion Golf Club was opened, and the monorail began servicing the course and bringing eager players to tackle the challenge of one of Ireland's most famous links courses. Here, a carriage from the monorail has been preserved by Michael Barry (photo: Irish Sporting Heritage).

Railway companies were important sponsors in the development of Irish sport in the nineteenth century. Here, the Great Southern and Western Railway offers cheap tickets to allow racegoers to attend the Cork Races (photo: Irish Sporting Heritage).

France for example, particularly rich in terms of architectural opulence or innovation. It is important, nevertheless, as each sporting site has a story to tell. They mirror political, economic and social trends in Ireland, they are the sites of sporting heroism, and they shift and change due to a host of external, non-sporting forces. They are all important and significant, although the scale will differ. The Real Tennis court in Dublin was built by a private individual, to cater for his needs and those limited numbers who followed such a minority sport. The Aviva Stadium is a national sporting site, catering for two of the biggest sports in Ireland and serving the needs of tens of thousands of supporters. Despite this difference in scale, both sites are over a century old, and tell stories of patronage, class, commercialism, politics, planning, design and ownership. They are architectural symbols of Ireland's sporting heritage, and while all such sites have and will continue to change and develop, this book encourages us to take a break in the play, and to open our eyes to the sporting sites that surround us.

The book is organised in three main sections. The first sets out a basic history of sport in Ireland, and seeks to contextualise the emergence of sporting sites as part of wider social, political and economic trends. The second focuses on a series of case studies of what might be termed major sites, that is, those that have regularly hosted international fixtures in their given sport, or else would be considered the national home or headquarters of the relevant association. The final two sections, and perhaps the most controversial, comprise a series of case studies of at least one important site connected with each of the major Irish sports, followed by a selection to illustrate a particular theme, such as workplace sports or temporary sporting facilities. These are controversial in that they are bound to spark debate. We have selected them on the basis of either their historical significance, architectural interest, or because the story of the site illustrates how historical change has impinged on a field of play. Many of the sites selected are Dublin centred: this is a product of the way Irish society and sport developed. The capital, with its abundant population, its growth of suburbs and its transport infrastructure, plus the fact that so many sporting bodies based themselves there, is simply home to many of the oldest and most significant sites. People will debate our choices and call to mind sites that they consider to have more significance: one they are a member of, have played at or been a spectator in. Part of the wider remit of this project was to create a database of sporting heritage sites across the island. It is available to view at www.irishsportingheritage.com, and for those who feel that our selections in the book can be added to, we encourage you to visit the website where details of your chosen site, photographs and other material you may have can be uploaded.

Overall we wish to emphasise how central sport, its sites and its heritage have been to the history of Ireland. Pick up most history books exploring the island's past, and sport barely rates a mention. The majority of scholars have always been more interested in the high culture of Ireland, produced predominantly by a literary metropolitan elite, than they have been in sporting life. Given that all social classes, in all parts of the island, have regularly played and watched sport since the later decades of the nineteenth century, and its central place in the contemporary daily narrative of the nation (there are not many subjects that warrant a supplement in the daily and weekend newspapers), the failure of sport to penetrate the consciousness of the majority of historians is surprising. And perhaps even sports followers are guilty of the same oversight. While most followers of sport will be up to date

LMS GOLF IN NORTHERN IRELAND
THE 8TH GREEN AT PORTRUSH
by
NORMAN WILKINSON, R.I.

Not only were the sporting attractions of Ireland for those on the island, but also those from afar. The London Midland and Scottish Railway company was a keen advocate of Ireland's sporting venues, such as Portrush Golf Course (photo: Irish Sporting Heritage).

with the sporting news of the day, and will have their own memory bank of great players and matches, how many of them pause to reflect on the historical significance of the stadium, venue or club they walk into? Why is the stadium where it is? Has it always been there? Has it changed over time? What kind of men and women have been here before?

Sport has, for the last century and a half, given the people of Ireland a series of pastimes and leisure pursuits, and in the process of playing, a built environment and a heritage has emerged. This book, and the project that accompanies it, asks you to take a moment, and consider those places where we have played, and where we continue to play.

2

HERITAGE IN IRELAND

WHEN A TOURIST CONSIDERS visiting Ireland, and contemplates what they may see, a host of images springs to mind. The landscape, especially that of the west, is evocative, as are ancient tales and legends, the great writers of the cultural revival, the GPO and other sites associated with political upheaval, pints of Guinness, traditional music and dancing, and the great buildings of Georgian Dublin. Indeed, for most Irish people, their list of important heritage and tourist sites would, but for some local variations, differ little. Certainly, with the exception of a visit to the GAA museum at Croke Park, there would be few, if any, sport-related sites on any inventory of Irish heritage or included in the plans of tourists. As this book makes clear, the sporting heritage of Ireland is significant, and it is one that tells a story of the Irish people and their past. Sport is not a minority pastime, but rather one that encompasses all regions, classes and religions. Why then, are sporting sites not often seen as important?

The 2002 *National Heritage Plan for Ireland* stated that, 'while our heritage is inextricably intertwined with our sense of identity, it also affirms the historic, cultural and natural inheritance which is shared on the island of Ireland'. The Plan goes on to argue that heritage should be preserved for present and future generations, as well as for tourists. It concluded that, 'our heritage is a presence which physically expresses the essence and the heartbeat of our collective historical identity'. The linking of heritage, and its preservation, to ideas of national identity and history, is not, however, unique to Ireland. In Britain, the National Trust and English Heritage care for a range of buildings from stately homes to industrial sites, while in the United States, the National Park Service manages sites ranging from the Grand Canyon to battlefields associated with the Revolution and the Civil War. In comparison to Britain and the US, Ireland has been a relative latecomer to the world of heritage. The Department of the Environment, Heritage and Local Government leads the government remit in caring for Ireland's heritage, and through Heritage Ireland manages a range of sites from Dublin Castle to Newgrange. The presentation of Irish heritage, and also to make use of it as an educational and tourist tool, is a comparatively recent phenomenon.

Although the need for a body overseeing Irish heritage was identified by a government committee in the early 1960s, it was not until 1988 that the National Heritage Council was established. The Council, funded by the National Lottery, is responsible for promoting heritage and carrying out research to support various organisations working on specific sites. As late as 2006, the Irish Heritage

The Fethard Hunt depicted in the early years of the twentieth century. Despite the banning of sports that were cruel to animals in the late nineteenth century, such as cock or dog fighting, the animal sports of the privileged classes were preserved (photo: National Library of Ireland).

Trust was established to care for historic houses and gardens across Ireland. In addition there are the various state museums and art galleries, as well as a network of county and local museums, archives and heritage associations, which care for smaller sites of local interest.

What is striking about the various bodies overseeing the care and promotion of Ireland's heritage is that their shared remit is quite traditional. Broadly speaking, Ireland's heritage, at the level of state and semi-state bodies, encapsulates three main areas: the landscape, ancient sites, and historic buildings and houses. Heritage Ireland, for example, cares for areas of outstanding beauty, such as the Connemara and Glenveagh National Parks, as well as buildings linked with the history of the nation, including Patrick Pearse's cottage in Rosmuc, County Galway, and Kilmainham Gaol in Dublin. The Irish Heritage Trust was established specifically to care for those historic, or 'big' houses associated with the Anglo-Irish tradition, and now manages properties such as Fota House, originally a hunting lodge for the Smith Barry family, in County Cork.

As with most heritage bodies around the world, those in Ireland work on restricted budgets, and hard decisions always have to be taken as to what can be preserved and put before the public. As a result, the focus has traditionally been on a range of buildings and sites that narrowly define Ireland's heritage. Sites associated with the elites of society and Ireland's tumultuous history of colonial struggle are favoured, whereas heritage that relates to the lower social orders, their lives and their working environments, are rarer. In this, preservation and heritage policies have often focused on what can be considered the 'high' or learned culture of Ireland. The National Museum, for example, has an extraordinarily rich collection of ancient artefacts, and yet in only one of its four sites, at the Museum of Country Life in Mayo, does it preserve and display objects from the type of rural life and work that the majority of Irish people endured in the past. Even the excellent National Inventory of Architectural Heritage, overseen by the Department of the Environment, Heritage and Local Government (www.buildingsofireland.ie), concentrates on buildings that are architecturally important (and often serviced an elite), rather than utilitarian structures that served the many. Its book on Sligo, for example, features churches, big houses, railway stations and lighthouses, amongst others, which display specific architectural styles or innovations. While the books include farmhouses, industrial mills and other buildings associated with the working classes, they are again more concerned with exploring the architectural vernacular than with what happened in these structures. The two sporting examples in Sligo, and sport has rarely featured in the whole inventory process at the national level, are Rosses Point Golf Club, built in 1894, and the Inishcrone Cliff Baths, built in 1890. Both of these buildings have particular varieties of late Victorian design that were deemed worthy of note and attention. None of this is to criticise the National Inventory, but to acknowledge that its definition of heritage is specific. The buildings included are illustrative of architectural styles from the past. Buildings with no architectural value, no matter how important their use to the wider society, are not included. This narrow definition of heritage is problematic for sporting sites in Ireland, as few are architecturally significant, and therefore slip below the radar of those who define heritage in terms of design aesthetics and historic building styles.

Despite the regular exclusion of sport and other forms of popular culture and working practices from definitions of heritage in Ireland, it is clear that when the public consume heritage, their focus and interests are often wider than what is on offer. Heritage that relates to the everyday or at least common experiences often has a greater resonance for many visitors than what is available on a visit

A bicycle race at the Gaelic Field in Shandon, Dungarvan, County Waterford. On the left of the photograph is Dan Fraher (the man kneeling with bowler hat and stick). He leased the field from Captain Richard Curran in 1885, and developed it into a sports field. On 31 March 1912 he acquired the sports field now known as the Fraher Field and which is one of the grounds used for Waterford County GAA games (photo: Waterford Museum).

Many sports and pastimes, such as swimming, used the natural environment. But even here, a built environment emerged, such as these changing huts at the women's bathing area in Portstewart, County Derry, in the late nineteenth century. Separation of the sexes was a common feature of bathing places across the country until the middle of the twentieth century (photo: National Library of Ireland).

Tennis parties were a common feature of upper class life in the last decade of the nineteenth century. Lawns within private estates and houses were rolled and marked out, a net and racquets purchased from a sports shop or by mail order, and friends invited. Such parties were socially exclusive and, as they were sporting events behind closed doors, both men and women would play. Such private courts and social groups were the genesis of formal tennis clubs in many areas (photo: National Library of Ireland).

to the 'big' house to see how the other half lived. Indeed, research has regularly shown that many visitors to the former homes of the privileged social classes were as interested in the lives of those who worked in such settings – the life below stairs – as they were in those privileged few who lived there. The difficulty for those in charge of Ireland's heritage is how they balance the need to care for historic sites and buildings with telling the story of the everyday. The houses of the elite, for example, while architecturally and historical significant, are hugely expensive to maintain and run. But at least their beauty and significance is obvious to all who visit. Far harder, in heritage terms, is how to convey the lived experience of the working classes. In England, living museums such as Ironbridge and Beamish, to name but two, have preserved the workshops and houses of the working classes, and through careful reconstruction and recreation, in the form of museum guides who dress and play the role of nineteenth-century workers, the everyday past is brought back to life. Ireland has struggled to recreate such an experience of the common life in its heritage sites. Where it has been achieved, at the Emigration museum in Cobh, for example, what is remembered and recreated is another example of Ireland's exceptionalism – mass emigration – rather than the everyday lives of people at home, in work and at play.

Of all the pulses and developments of everyday life that came to the fore in the late nineteenth century, and was shared (albeit in different venues) across classes, none was more vibrant than sport. It is a passion that is still alive today and is something that has created a wealth of history and heritage across the island. The aim of this book is to explore sporting heritage, which we argue has been ignored by national heritage policies and, with the occasional exception, the administering bodies of sport. The latter point is important. Sporting bodies exist, and have always functioned, to make their particular games happen. The monies they receive in gate receipts, government grants or membership fees are dedicated to pitches, infrastructure, salaries and so on. So while sporting associations may be the keepers of their sport's past and history, they are often more concerned with the practical daily business of making sport take place than preserving the past. Also, while heritage, in the form of the built environment, museums or archives, should be part of the remit of sporting bodies, we acknowledge that the support of such can often be impractical (architecturally significant buildings do not necessarily conform to the sporting demands of today), or else expensive and unlikely to produce profit (museums, for example, are important for conveying a message about what an association stands for and why its past is significant, but they are not commercial entities that can easily produce a positive revenue stream).

As the book will show, sporting sites are not necessarily important for their architectural styles or the magnificence of the building, but rather are important venues for mass social activity. Sporting heritage sites have housed, and continue to do so, a variety of games and sports, played by all classes in a mixture of settings. It is a heritage that everyone will recognise as familiar and one, we argue, that is as important to understand as the ancient, political and elite sites that are usually preserved and visited. If we can understand, as we attempt to do in this book, why sporting heritage is important to our shared history, and gain some sense of what it is and how it can be identified and (where necessary or practical) be preserved, then perhaps in the future planning of Ireland's heritage strategies, discussions of sporting sites may enter the equation.

Right: Many examples of sporting heritage in Ireland are actually monuments and plaques celebrating sporting heroes, sites and events. In 2011, for example, a plaque was unveiled marking the house on Clare Street in Dublin where George Sigerson lived. Amongst his many activities, Sigerson was a keen advocate of Gaelic football in a college setting, and he donated the cup that would bear his name, and is still competed for a century later (photo: Irish Sporting Heritage).

Below: The Shannon Rowing Club building in Limerick is one of the few protected sporting structures in Ireland. The clubhouse was designed in the Edwardian Arts and Crafts idiom by the architect William Clifford Smith. The builders were Messrs Gough. The variation of the fenestration and the contrasting façade finishes at each level provide architectural interest to the maritime heritage of the city. The Shannon Rowing Club was founded by Sir Peter Tait in 1868 (picture: Damien Murphy).

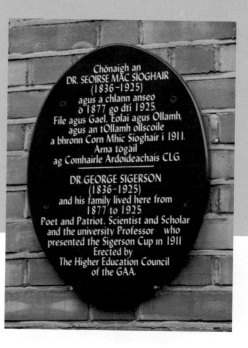

3

SPORT AND SOCIETY

IRELAND, like many nations, has always been a place of sport. As Neil Tranter observed, 'from the dawn of human civilisation, it seems, the need for some form of sporting physical recreation has almost been as imperative to human beings as the need to procreate, work and eat'. In Ireland, whether in the form of traditional games such as hurling, throwing weights or folk football, the seasons, and most importantly, high days and holidays, were celebrated and marked by sporting contests. To the modern eye many of these traditional contests would seem unruly, without a referee or any agreed code of conduct, but sports they were. Sport or, more descriptively, physical contest, be it throwing or kicking a ball, racing or contests of strength, was always something that the Irish, along with most Europeans, took to during the various seasons and holidays. The games might be driven by the desires of high-rolling gamblers, landlords seeking to entertain their tenants, or agricultural workers looking to amuse themselves on a day off, but all were about physical contest, fun and frivolity. The key historical point is that these were games that were not organised around a regular season, a cup competition or league structure: they were not codified in the way we would understand contemporary sport. Sports prior to the late nineteenth century were localised, infrequent, devoid of structure, relatively low in

participation and violent. In short, they would be unrecognisable to the sports followers of today.

In the nineteenth century, the middle and upper classes began to examine the games that were played and they did not like what they saw. In an age of rationality and organisation, the leisure time of people seemed chaotic and disorganised: bull running, bear baiting and dog fighting, all flew in the face of Victorian rationality. There was a disconnection between Enlightenment physicality and the games that people played. The middle and upper classes in Britain, much of Europe, in the United States and across the fast growing cities of the British Empire, began to eschew the games and sports of the eighteenth and early nineteenth centuries – which they felt were disorganised and degenerative – and instead looked towards strictly organised team sports that stressed values that sat alongside the mores of the society in which they lived. As a result the team games of cricket, soccer and rugby, amongst others, came to the fore. These were sports which were regulated by a central body, and which had strict rules and regulations. They governed not only the size of the playing field and the numbers of players, but also how the competitors should conduct themselves. From the playing fields of Eton and Rugby and various other English public schools and universities, a code emerged as to how the

games should be played and, most importantly, how the players should behave. The Victorian age witnessed a wholesale codification, organisation and regulation of sport. Where before there had been local sports and traditions, in their place came a fixed and regulated sense of the rules: games became sports, and everything was defined. Pitches, the length of the game, numbers on each team, the scoring process, the role of the referee, the league or cup structures, the timing of the season, and the absolute power of the governing body: everything was made standard, and all was rigorously enforced. This chapter will examine developments, mainly in Britain, to understand how codified sport first evolved, and what this meant for the production of a built heritage around grounds and pitches. Ireland's sporting history, while sharing many common elements with other developed nations, is at certain levels quite distinct. It is necessary to understand the more common British, European and North American expansion of a built sporting environment, so the unique points of the Irish case can best be understood.

The power of the movements in society that led to the birth of 'modern' sport can be seen in the short timescale in which the major games became codified. In Britain, the Football Association was formed in 1863, the Rugby Football Union in 1871, the Amateur Athletics Association in 1880 and the Rowing Association in 1882. Such developments and codifications were mirrored in Ireland with the founding of the Irish Rugby Football Union in 1874, the Irish Football Association in 1880 and even the avowedly anti-colonial Gaelic Athletic Association in 1884.

So why did modern sport emerge in Ireland and elsewhere in such a relatively small period of Victorian history? The key issues were modernisation, industrialisation, urbanisation and a transport revolution. In Britain, the industrial revolution produced wholesale changes in the ways that many people lived their lives. Rather than existing in rural areas, with their lives governed by the length of the day, the passing of the seasons and the needs of their crops and animals, people found their lives transformed by the industrial revolution. Industrialisation created factories governed by strict working hours, towns and cities that housed the workers in close proximity and a transport network (first canals, and later railways) sprang up to move people and goods.

In the new towns of the north and midlands of England, as well as in South Wales and the dockyards of Scotland and Belfast, a mass of people employed in industrial work came together. Their working hours were strictly regimented and, in due course, so were the hours that they would have for leisure. Rather than a six-day week, most employees, in response to socially enlightened legislation passed in Parliament (the 1850 Factor Act and its successors ended the working day at 2 p.m. on Saturdays), switched to a five-and-a-half-day week, and suddenly the worker's Saturday afternoons were free. Into the void of Saturday leisure time, especially for men, came sport. The upper and self-improving middle classes had realised the value of sport – both physical and moral – in the public schools that dominated privileged education in the mid-nineteenth century. At first it had been cricket, followed by rugby, and games such as lacrosse. The main issue was the value of team spirit, the leadership of a captain and the ideologies of fair play and gentlemanly conduct. For many factory owners of the later nineteenth century, driven by a spirit of Victorian (and often

Facing page: Now illegal in Ireland, otter hunting was a popular blood sport at the end of the nineteenth century amongst the landed elite. This image from 1901 shows the hunters and dogs of Curraghmore pursuing an otter through a river. Watching the hunt from a carriage or on horseback was a central part of the social side of the day, and spectators can be seen watching from the bridge (photo: National Library of Ireland).

Protestant) paternalism, the value of organising sport for their workers was a way of enhancing their core morality and improving their fitness. Most important in the emergence of large-scale, factory-based sports were those industrialists with a strong sense of social and moral responsibility, such as the Bourneville factory in Birmingham and Port Sunlight on Merseyside, both of which provided their workers with good quality housing, education, healthcare and comprehensive sporting facilities. On a less impressive scale in terms of facilities, but important for the geographical spread of sporting facilities in England were both the Church of England and the Catholic Church, with many clubs, such as the rugby playing Wakefield Trinity, having their origins as Church teams.

In the second half of the nineteenth century, factory owners, as well as local publicans and hoteliers looking for extra trade, began sponsoring Saturday afternoon sport. From such an entrepreneurial spirit, soccer and rugby league teams emerged. They were professional or semi-professional, and the goal was to fill the afternoon of the workers – the paying spectators – with a sport to watch or play, and in the process, make money. For those sponsoring the games, they had a crowd of workers who were occupied, entertained and spending the small amount of money they reserved for their leisure. The supporters were buying into the sense of community provided by supporting their representative team and were also spending money getting to and watching the games, as well as enjoying some pre- and post-match entertainment and consumption. For the sponsors of the sport, the railway companies, hotel owners and publicans, the spending around the match provided them with profit.

In Britain, where industrialisation hit a critical mass and involved millions of workers, the sporting revolution produced professional leagues in soccer and rugby league, as well as the mixed professional-amateurism of cricket and the working class passion for rugby union in the mining and steel towns of South Wales. Equally, boxing became hugely popular from the 1880s and 1890s, once workers could afford the sixpence admission charge. These all became, at local and national level, big business, with thriving leagues and cup competitions. The substantial crowds that flocked to such competitions created an income for those who owned the grounds and the teams, and as a result, they began building stadia so that crowds could be accommodated and charged accordingly. The larger the stadium, the larger the potential income from gate receipts. In the years either side of the First World War, the elite soccer teams of England and Scotland began constructing expansive, purpose-built stadia, and certain architects and engineers, such as Archibald Leitch, built a series of grounds for football teams such as Arsenal, Manchester United, Aston Villa, Liverpool and Everton. New building materials in the 1910s and 1920s, such as reinforced concrete, allowed wooden stands to be replaced by two-tier steel and concrete stands which, in turn, ushered in higher capacities and great comfort for spectators. Many of these stands, indeed the grounds as a whole, were seen as iconic and architecturally significant. However, with the crowd-related disasters at Heysel (in Brussels), Hillsborough and Bradford in the 1980s and 1990s, the view was taken that the soccer grounds of Britain were outmoded and dangerous. While many clubs decided to relocate from old fashioned grounds based in densely populated areas to new state-of-the-art grounds, such as Bolton Wanderers' switch from Burnden Park to the Reebok Stadium (after a 102-year residency in the former), others such as Liverpool and Manchester United have built new stands within the confines of their existing grounds. Perhaps the most significant preservation of soccer-related heritage took place in north London. When Arsenal decided to leave their iconic, art deco style ground of Highbury and move to the Emirates Stadium, the fact that Highbury was a listed building meant that the club worked with developers to transform the old stands into apartment blocks, thereby preserving the splendour of Archibald Leitch's design.

Of perhaps greater importance to the built sporting environment in Britain and elsewhere was the plethora of private sporting clubs that sprang up in the years on either side of 1900. Although golf (the British Open from 1860), tennis (Wimbledon from 1877) and cricket (the Ashes from 1877), all have top-level competitions that attract paying crowds, their strength in terms of numbers came from the emergence of private clubs across Britain. Given that these clubs were socially exclusive and attracted the middle and upper class members of the new professional elites in urban areas, facilities were readily bought, and money raised to build clubhouses. In Britain, many of these structures, as evidenced by the English Heritage series *Played in Britain* (www.playedinbritain.co.uk) were of such sumptuousness and architectural significance that many of them are now listed structures. Tennis, for example, began life as an adaptation of real tennis, conjured up by one Major Walter Wingfield in 1873. Such was the success of his vision for a game that could be played on the lawn (as opposed to a custom-built court) that he began selling boxed sets that included racquets, balls and a net, plus instructions for marking out a court. For a rising middle class, the game was perfect. It could be played in the confines of one's own home, and could include both men and women without fear of social outrage. Tennis parties were a central part of the social scene in Britain and the United States in the 1870s and 1880s and such was their success that people began formalising such parties into official clubs. These clubs spread across Britain rapidly, covering the country from Edgbaston in Birmingham (1875), Chapel Allerton in Leeds (1880) and Rustlings in Sheffield (1883). All of these clubs, and those that joined them, erected basic pavilions for use as changing facilities,

In the early decades of the twentieth century, the most compelling sports for many spectators were those that embraced the modernity of speed and the motor engine. Motor bike and car races became spectacles attended by thousands, as with this race in Limerick (photo: Limerick City Archives).

built courts and expanded over the years. Built to provide practical comfort, the buildings in many private clubs were more than utilitarian structures and were not concerned with profit maximisation in the same way as a soccer stadium. As such, the clubhouses and surroundings of the private club often had an opulence and level of architectural innovation that spoke to the wealth of those who joined and patronised such establishments.

In addition to sporting associations and private clubs, a range of institutions was also important in spreading sport throughout Britain and beyond and in the process producing a further branch of built sporting environment. These included schools, universities, churches, hospitals, factories, the military and

so on. Each of these institutions provided sporting facilities for those they employed or for whom they had responsibility. Many of these facilities were basic, simply a field to play on, and were often temporary. Others, however, were built grandly. In privileged schools across Britain, the facilities that were built in places such as Rugby, Harrow, Eton and Winchester remain some of the most iconic and historic locations where sport takes place. These institutions were also central in the spread of sport from Britain. The British military and civil service had a presence across the British Empire, and wherever they found themselves, they played sport. Much work has been carried out on the diffusion of sports across the globe and it is the machinery of the British Empire which left the deepest legacy. Not only did it carry the games of rugby and cricket, most notably, to modern-day India, Pakistan,

Nowadays, sports grounds, especially those which attract large numbers of spectators, operate under strict health and safety regulations. In the early decades of sport such rules did not exist, and temporary stands were thrown up quickly for one-off or occasional events. This was particularly true for horse racing, as evidenced by this wooden stand for ladies and their partners at Duncannon Races in the late nineteenth century (photo: National Library of Ireland).

Golf clubs nowadays are usually serviced by a comfortable clubhouse featuring a bar, restaurant, changing room and pro shop. When the early courses were established late in the nineteenth century, such luxuries were often unimaginable. Also, those who worked at the club – golf professionals and groundsmen – were not included in the planning of any buildings for the members. They had to put up with the most basic facilities, as with this shed for the groundsman of the St Anne's Club in Dublin (photo: National Library of Ireland).

As stadia were developed into the twentieth century, so terraces and other facilities for spectators were constructed. One addition that was common across most GAA, rugby and soccer grounds was the scoreboard. Varying in style, size and technological innovation, many remained very basic. Cavan's county ground at Breffni Park was opened in 1923. The photograph shows the hand-painted signage on the scoreboard being kept up to date by young volunteers (photo: Johnston Central Library).

Opened in 2010, the new stand at Galway Racecourse is a state of the art facility that comes into its own during Galway Race Week. While used for only a few days each year, the stand demonstrates how modern design mixes contemporary architecture with the needs of racegoers, diners and corporate sponsors (picture: Galway Racecourse).

Alongside those institutions that chose to provide sporting facilities there was also an important mandatory creation of pitches, pools and so on, by the state in Britain. One of the great legacies of British welfare attitudes was the large-scale public provision of sporting facilities from the late nineteenth century. Although this provision has been under constant threat in recent decades, as local councils seek to balance their books, the range of sporting facilities provided by the public purse is impressive. Councils were mandated by a series of laws to provide sporting places for the British public. The drive behind this provision was not always altruistic and was often the product of concerns over health and hygiene (especially the provision of public baths and swimming pools) or else concerns, especially in light of the poor physical condition of conscripts into the army during the Anglo-Boer War of 1899–1902, over the fitness of the British nation. Other bodies – such as the Central Council for Physical Recreation, which has, since the 1930s, supported the public provision of sport – have been vociferous in their advocacy of school sport, and places in which people, especially urban dwellers, can play. Although the impulses behind public provision may have changed, it is interesting to note that one of the largest anticipated legacies of the London 2012 Olympics is a massive increase in the public uptake of sporting activity.

What has been set out here is a brief outline of how sporting facilities and infrastructures developed in Britain. Many of the catalysts for the development of sport, and sporting sites, are mirrored in Ireland, but others, such as a century-old support of public provision, is lacking. What is also notable is the comparative lack of architectural innovation in sporting facilities. This is not to say that Ireland does not have a rich sporting heritage, but rather to flag the fact that it is significantly different from that of Britain. Across the Irish Sea, sporting heritage is

South Africa, Australia, New Zealand and the Caribbean nations, but once introduced, the institutions of those countries began to duplicate British sporting practice. Wealth, as elsewhere, was an issue but for the sons of upper class colonial Indians or South Africans, the games they played at school, although eventually adapted so that they became sports representing the nation, were British.

predominantly concerned with a built heritage, much of which dates back to the era of Victorian splendour and municipal opulence in public buildings. Ireland did not have, with the exception perhaps of Belfast, a Victorian building boom akin to most British provincial cities. So, while sport was developing at roughly the same time in Ireland, it did not have the same philanthropic and municipal building programmes to house sporting activity. What is important in Ireland, as we will explain, is that Ireland's sporting heritage is more often about the history of the sporting site and its social history narrative, rather than its architectural significance.

Many sports have used the natural landscape as their playing field or their backdrop. Cliff diving is one such sport, and here, in 2009, Orlando Duque dives off the cliffs of Inis Mór (photo: Ray Dernski, Red Bull Content Pool).

4

SPORT
IN IRELAND

THE YEARS OF THE GREAT FAMINE, 1845–1849, and the resultant emigration hugely dislocated Irish society. Despite the upheavals, the damaging effects of the Famine were uneven and, for many, life went on as normal. Also, the wider processes of modernisation, which were such a feature of the Victorian era, continued to change Ireland. Railways were built, industry grew and the process of urbanisation, despite the loss of population, continued. In the midst of all these macro changes, sport continued to be played and developed anew. In the pre-Famine decades, traditional sports held sway in many parts of the country: hurling was popular, animal sports, whether fighting with cocks and dogs, and bare-knuckle (or prize) fighting, remained a staple diet for many. Cricket was rapidly growing in popularity, and water sports, whether yachting, rowing or fishing, made a clear mark on suitable landscapes. Horse racing also grew quickly, and many of the tracks in Ireland saw the first built environments for sport develop at this time.

After the mid-nineteenth century, modern or codified sports, diffused from Britain, began to enter Ireland. The movement of people between Ireland and Britain has always been a major feature of the relationship between the two countries. Whether industrialists, seasonal workers, schoolchildren or students, many individuals regularly crossed to Britain for a period of time before returning home for their holidays, to restart their lives or after they had completed their professional training or education. It is with these travellers that modern sport moved and, for example, the first soccer club – Cliftonville in Belfast – was formed in Ireland in 1879 by John McAlery, after he had seen a game in Scotland while on honeymoon. Schoolboys who had been sent to elite schools in England played new games, such as rugby, and on returning home encouraged their friends to play with them. Likewise, such boys, once studying as university students in Dublin or Cork, found enough like-minded sports enthusiasts to form some of the first clubs in an Irish setting (e.g. Dublin University Football Club at Trinity College in 1854). Class and social elitism were also important in propagating the enthusiasm for the sporting revolution. Hunting, an elite pastime par excellence, became an ever more social event and, with that switch, so the number of hunts grew. Cricket continued its spread across the country and in the industrial northeast, working-class sports such as soccer developed rapidly from the first toehold in Belfast.

While some of the larger stadia in the country are designed by specialist architects and built by experienced firms, many smaller grounds in the country, particularly in the GAA, are the products of local builders, community fund-raising and volunteer effort. This is the stand in Rosmuc's Na Piarsaigh stadium that serves as the shared home ground for the teams of Rosmuc, Camus and An Sraith Salach (photo: Irish Sporting Heritage).

In the switch from pre-modern to modern sport, some traditional games survived. Horseshoe pitching is a game with a long history, which now survives as a network of local clubs organised under the auspices of the Horseshoe Pitchers Association of Ireland. Here, on the banks of the River Dodder in Dublin, a small sign and horseshoe attached to a tree announce the presence of the local club (photo: Irish Sporting Heritage).

This picture, taken in the first decade of the twentieth century on a golf course in County Louth, shows two seemingly overdressed women tackling their round. Golf was an important private club sport which, while excluding many people on the grounds of wealth, was also an important place for middle and upper class women to play sport (photo: National Library of Ireland).

Now the town's marketplace, the Wexford Bull Ring was operated by the local butcher's guild between 1621 and 1710, with the hides of the killed bulls being presented to the town's mayor. A sport very much disapproved of by the voices of Enlightenment, bull baiting was an early victim of moves towards rational sporting pastimes (photo: Wexford County Library).

The development of sport in Ireland, however, was not simply a process that aped and duplicated what had happened in Britain. There were clear differences between the two countries, and these – whether issues of infrastructure, class, religion, politics, business or geography – all had an impact on the Irish sporting landscape. In Ireland, the process of modernisation, in the form of an industrial revolution, never matched the scale of Britain, and where it did occur, in Belfast, Cork, Dublin and Limerick, it was patchy and incomplete. However, the transport revolution in Ireland was carried out at a similar level to Great Britain, and towns and villages were linked across the country by rail. Ireland lacked the types of privileged educational institutions that Britain had but still had a network of Catholic and Church of Ireland schools that were patronised by the rising middle class. In these schools, as well as amongst those Irish boys sent to Britain for their education, the spirit of sport was hugely important, and the Leinster Schools Cup began as early as 1877. These boys and young men, as a result of their schooling and because of their university years at Trinity or the Queens' Colleges, were the agents for much sporting diffusion in Ireland.

Once the sporting revolution began in Ireland, despite the high levels of emigration that continued in the wake of the mid-century famine and the regular social upheavals caused by national politics or the battles over land ownership, it laid deep roots. At first, the games that succeeded in winning a following were those based on imports from Britain. Cricket was probably the most popular team game in Ireland until the 1890s, and athletics, which built on aspects of Irish traditionalism, such as weight throwing, was hugely popular with competitors and spectators. Soccer, after first having been imported to the northeast, spread to Dublin (Dublin Association Football Club formed in 1883), Cork

Cricket was a popular game across Ireland until the late nineteenth century. With the upheavals associated with the Land War and the advent of the GAA, many culturally minded Catholics abandoned the game. Cricket retreated into an ever-smaller number of social settings where the game's imperial ties were not seen as problematic. This game at Mourne Grange School, Kilkeel, County Down, took place just after the First World War (photo: National Library of Ireland).

(Crosshaven AFC founded in 1898) and many other towns and cities and found a following amongst the army, manual workers, clerks and shop assistants. Rugby, while more elitist, and having its major strength in schools, colleges and old boys' associations, gathered support in a series of regular cup competitions and in Limerick, due to local patronage, spread beyond its usual class confines to become the game of working class people.

Throughout the 1880s and 1890s, as modern sport spread across Ireland, the various games became more standardised and the power of the central regulating body more important. Once everyone involved understood the common rules and joined the national body, games, challenge matches, cup competitions and leagues became easier to organise. With a critical mass of games and matches to play, if you were an athlete, or to watch, if you were a spectator, so the business associated with sport developed. Where once there had been a traditional sport organised for a religious holiday, there developed a regular season of matches and fixtures. From regularity (and income) sprang physical sites on which sport could be played week in and week out.

Bowling clubs were formed in Ireland in the 1890s and proved popular in many parts of the country. The Ballymena club in County Antrim was founded in 1904 and quickly secured its own green, which is depicted here shortly after foundation (photo: National Library of Ireland).

Cycling was one of the boom pastimes and sports of the late nineteenth century in Ireland, and popular amongst both sexes. As with many sports, businesses came to the fore to supply the eager adherents. The Rudge Whitworth cycle manufacturers were founded in Britain in 1894, and opened their Dublin shop on St Stephen's Green shortly after. (Photo: National Library of Ireland)

As sport established itself as a major concern for people across Ireland, irrespective of class, commercial opportunities arose for those prepared to sponsor sports events or build facilities for members or spectators. Golf and tennis are classic examples of games that organised themselves as private clubs based around a paying membership, while others, such as racing, soccer and rugby, for example, saw their commercial future in erecting stands in order to charge admission fees to spectators. Major events, such as race and athletics meetings, which attracted large crowds, became associated with railway companies. These offered trophies in their own name for the winners of a given event, while also offering spectators discounted fares so that they could attend. In addition to using local stations that were near to events, railway companies also built stations and platforms adjacent to sporting sites, such as the railway stop next to the Curragh racecourse or beside Woodenbridge golf course. These were not altruistic constructions. They were built to make money from those who wanted to watch and play sport.

With the realisation that sport was a spectacle people would pay to watch, so grounds became enclosed. Rather than being played in a farmer's field that lay fallow for the season, clubs began purchasing or leasing their own grounds. To facilitate paid entrance, and hence a revenue, clubs began roping off the playing surface and constructing rudimentary entrance ways or turnstiles. As crowds increased and the expectations of the paying customer rose, so terraces and stands were erected to facilitate better viewing, and perimeter walls were constructed so that only those who paid could watch.

The establishment of the Gaelic Athletic Association in 1884 had a revolutionary effect on the nature of Irish sport, due to its cultural nationalism, its amateurism and volunteer ethos. However, while the GAA, and in particular its ban on 'foreign' games, may have dented the popularity of games such as cricket, it did not alter the progress and development of sporting sites, grounds and facilities. Rather, the GAA became another sporting organisation that sought to purchase grounds, build stands, clubhouses and other facilities to house its members, followers and spectators. By the end of the nineteenth century, after three decades of development, Irish life and its landscape had been changed by the advent of a sporting revolution. Where before there had been transitory and occasional sporting fixtures of a traditional nature, played on temporary pitches, there was now modern sport, with its regular fixture list, mass spectator following and participant interest, mostly housed in purpose-built facilities. Changes in working practices and greater access to leisure time, accompanied by a transport revolution in the form of the railways, and the sporting ethos of educational establishments, had breathed life into sport. Once these sports were established, and the crowds and players came to watch and take part, so a built environment emerged to house them. Ireland's sporting heritage, in the form of grounds, stands, terraces, clubhouses, pitches and courses had been born.

Despite the arrival of modern sport into Ireland by the end of the nineteenth century, and the local conditions that shaped it, much remained contested and complex. These ongoing issues would have a huge impact on sport and its physical spaces into the twentieth century and beyond.

All sports have a certain constituency of followers and participants. Affiliation to any given sport can be the product of our schooling, local provision or simply by choice. Despite the ubiquitous nature of sports coverage in the media these days, and the fact that many sports fans will follow a multitude of sports, there are some that people may feel excluded from or are uninterested in. These exclusions are the products of history and in Ireland the reasons behind them are complex. Cricket was, until the

Tolka Park, now the home of Shelbourne FC, was built in the 1950s in Drumcondra. It is a classic urban soccer stadium, and is penned in on all sides by residential development. Despite the property boom of the Celtic Tiger years, the ground was not relocated, and remains as part of the urban landscape of inner north city Dublin (photo: Damien Murphy).

1890s, probably the most popular game in Ireland, in terms of player numbers and matches contested. This popularity was due, in part, to the game's ability to appeal to all classes. While there were subtle class distinctions on the field of play, a team could encompass the local landowner, members of the professions, as well as publicans, blacksmiths and agricultural workers. With the advent of the Land War in the 1880s, and later the emergence of the GAA, such cosy class intermingling fractured. Cricket, rather than being seen as a game for all, was dismissed by the GAA as a garrison game, and the stereotype (whether true or not) of who played it began to encompass only social elites and Protestants. Cricket is perhaps the most extreme example of a sport that appealed widely being destroyed by the process of identifying games with specific socio-economic, religious and national groups.

In Britain, the United States, Australia and many European countries, the choices about which games people play (and, by proxy, with whom particular games are identified), while complex, are essentially products of class and geography. In Ireland, the dividing points around sporting choices were far wider. Class, or rather access to money, determined who followed certain sports. Where

Left: The troubles in the north of Ireland disrupted the smooth running of sport at many levels. One of the most famous cases was the partial occupation of the Crossmaglen Rangers ground by the British army. While the club continued its games under the shadow of one of the busiest army bases in the North, the issue was rancorous and often raised in the Dáil and the House of Commons (photo: GAA Museum and Archives).

Facing page: Nowadays sport takes many forms, and the rise of extreme sports has been a notable feature of recent years. One-off events in this area, sponsored by Red Bull, have become hugely popular, with spectacular sports mixed with impressive landscapes and landmark buildings. In 2010, the Red Bull Steeple Cross was raced around the grounds of Buttevant Castle, County Cork (photo: Predrag Vuckovic, Red Bull Content Pool).

the organising unit was the private club, necessitating an annual membership fee, inclusion and exclusion were determined by wealth or the lack of it. As a result, games such as golf, tennis, croquet, and hockey were dominated by the middle and upper classes. Sports that required wealth to take part in, such as horse racing, were favoured by the social elite, but the attractions of the fairground atmosphere and gambling opportunities afforded by race days meant that the appeal of racing, in terms of spectatorship, was much wider. Yet, in the building of stands and enclosures, the organisers of racing ensured that social divisions and hierarchies were enforced.

Perceptions of political and religious identity have also shaped Irish sport to a great degree. The GAA tied itself, in its early decades, to a support of cultural and political nationalism. In introducing its various bans, the GAA produced a sporting organisation that, while central to definitions of community across the country, effectively excluded Protestants, most problematically in the north of the country. Soccer was a game that developed in the industrial northeast, and found its most ardent followers in similar urban environments elsewhere. As a game, it has struggled to spread beyond major conurbations, and its following has largely been in working class areas.

Some sports have appealed widely, such as fishing or swimming, but even here there are lines drawn that separate people. Fishing, a hugely popular sport, encompasses the urban dweller fishing from the banks of

the local canal or river, right through to the country gentleman who fly fishes on private estates. Swimming, while a highly popular sport and pastime, was until the 1960s, hampered by a lack of facilities. Unlike the UK, whose welfare state system encouraged the public provision of swimming facilities, in the Republic of Ireland the public purse turned its attention to public provision only in the 1960s. Swimming pools were often available in holiday towns in Ireland, such as Bray, County Wicklow, or else were the products of the natural environment, such as the Forty Foot in Dalkey, County Dublin. Yet even here, exclusions were a feature. Until a campaign aimed at winning equality began in the 1970s, the Forty Foot was strictly a men-only facility. Access to sporting sites has often been predicated on gender, and even recently the battle lines were drawn over women's membership at the male bastion of Portmarnock Golf Club.

Schools and colleges have a huge impact on sporting choices, and the provision of facilities in schools for certain sports often determines the sporting loyalty of people for their lifetime. While schools increasingly provide a wide variety of sporting choices for their pupils, many institutions are closely identified in the public mind as rugby or GAA schools. These choices do not necessarily follow a uniform religious pattern in which, for example, Catholic schools all play Gaelic games; indeed Leinster schools rugby is dominated by the top private Catholic schools.

Some of the biggest challenges to sport have been in the form of the political upheavals that affected Ireland in the twentieth century. During the revolutionary period, in the first quarter of the twentieth century, many sports became defined by their perceived religious affiliations, and the partition of the country led to clear lines being drawn.

Some such as the GAA and rugby remained 32-county organisations, while others such as soccer divided along the border. During the revolutionary period, the traditional role that the garrison had played in Irish sporting life was destroyed. Those members of the Anglo-Irish elite and the Church of Ireland often retreated into private clubs, where they could pursue their sports unhindered by questions of identity and free from criticism or attack. The period of the modern troubles in the North further divided sport along sectarian lines, and the disappearance of Belfast Celtic in 1949 and Derry City in 1972 from Northern Irish soccer spoke volumes about the complexities of sporting identity. In the North, the provision of sporting facilities was a deeply divisive question, with the Stormont administration and many unionist local councils refusing to support the GAA in its search for grounds. Also, given the close links between Protestantism and the unionism that dominated the North until the onset of the peace process, the question of playing on Sunday, something the GAA regularly did, was seen as deeply problematic. Even when British laws changed to allow a host of commercial sports, such as racing, to take place on Sunday, Down Royal remained, until recently, firmly closed.

Clearly there are a host of other issues that have shaped Ireland's sporting landscape, and there is far more detail and nuance than space allows for here. The critical point, however, is that all sporting sites in Ireland are not simply products of someone's desire to play. They are certainly the creation of sporting impulses, but also of social, political and economic factors that were, and in many ways remain, unique to Ireland. To understand how a sports ground or club looks today is to shed light on the wider history of Ireland.

5

INFRASTRUCTURE

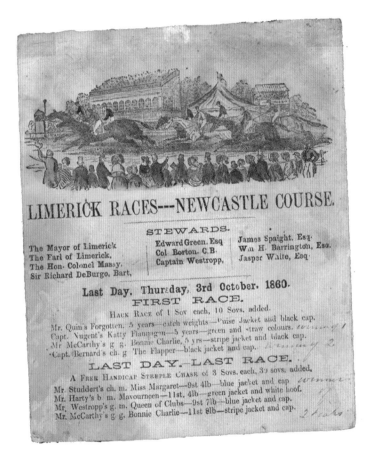

As the railway companies spread their networks across Ireland in the second half of the nineteenth century, so sporting events came to benefit from increased attendance afforded by ease of accessibility. This poster for the Limerick Races in October 1860 is highly stylised, yet illustrates the size of the stands and facilities available at this early date (photo: Limerick City Archives).

SPORT, as we understand it today, is a product of modernity. While there had long been sports and games practised in Ireland and elsewhere prior to the mid-nineteenth century, these can be understood as pre-modern. In the second half of the nineteenth century the world changed dramatically, and a series of revolutions in industry, transport and technology, amongst others, hastened the pace of societal change. A sport simply existing is not enough for it to be successful, and to become popular. Players and spectators need to travel to games, everyone has to understand the rules and scoring, there has to be a large enough population to embrace sport, people have to be made aware of the sports that are taking place, and they have to be able to source the necessary equipment and grounds for them to take to the field. This may sound obvious, but they are critical considerations. Irish sport in the first half of the nineteenth century, while taking place, was often restricted to periods of holidays and fairs. The games that were played at these times were traditional, but essentially one off. They were played on impromptu grounds, with large, disorganised teams taking to the field. Sports, in this context, were more carnival-esque than codified. Some sports, such as horse racing, cricket and even hurling, did take place on a more regular basis, but these were different as they relied on wealth and patronage. In horse racing, for example, it was landowners who had the means to own and race horses and, critically, the estates

The GAA was perhaps the greatest sporting beneficiary of the railway network, as it allowed supporters to travel from parish to parish, county to county and across the country. This poster from 1935 is typical in that it not only promotes the game, but offers detailed information on fares, routes and times from Donegal into Dublin (photo: Irish Sporting Heritage).

hurling, while played predominantly by rural workers prior to the establishment of the GAA, patronage was key. The men who played the games did not have the means to access fields for play. As a result they were dependant on the generosity of a landowner who would lend them a field. Such ad hoc arrangements, while allowing people to play, did not produce the necessary stability and frequency of fixtures to produce the regularity that is demanded of modern league and cup competitions.

So while there is a nascent sense of sport in Ireland prior to the Famine, there is no sense that what existed was comparable to what we understand as modern, codified sport. While sporting associations and federations were the key to producing rules and regulations, there was a whole series of other factors on which the success and popularity of sport would depend. This infrastructure, which would support the spread and growth of sport, emerged from the 1860s and would be critical in turning Ireland into a sporting nation and, in turn, creating the built environment around the sporting sites under consideration here.

One of the great advancements of the nineteenth century was the advent of the railways, the network of which spread across Ireland. The first railway in Ireland, fully completed in 1834, linked Dublin with Kingstown (Dun Laoghaire) and, from then on, the network spread rapidly, reaching its peak at the end of the nineteenth century. Railways allowed sporting competitors and spectators to travel easily and cheaply across large distances to take part in and watch sporting fixtures. The ability to travel had a huge impact on the development of sport and many sporting sites developed precisely because they were serviced by a railway line. This was especially true of many racecourses, a good number of which had their own station for services on race day, and also many golf courses. Even a sport such as angling was aware of the power of the

on which to mark out a course. While race meetings were open to the public, they relied almost entirely on the efforts of wealthy men allowing access to their lands. The same was true of cricket which, although drawing its players from across the classes, again depended on the patronage of the wealthy who would put aside a portion of their estate to prepare a wicket and even build a pavilion. Again in

Woodenbridge Station was opened in 1885 as a stop on the Dublin-to-Rosslare line. While having a multitude of uses, its most noticeable customers were those travelling with their golf bags. Across the tracks from the station stood the entrance and clubhouse of Woodenbridge Golf Club, which opened its doors in 1894. The station officially closed in 1964, but it still stands at the entrance to the club (photo: National Library of Ireland).

This map, produced in 1916, demonstrates the clear relationship between sporting sites and the railways. While there are a few clubs at a short distance from a rail line, the vast majority are adjacent to them. Put simply, the railway map of Ireland dictated, in large part, the sporting (and here, the golfing) map of the country (photo: from Harold White, *The Irish Golfing Guide* for 1916 (Dublin: Irish Life, 1916)).

Left: The railway network in Ireland, at the beginning of the twentieth century, was extensive. Shown here in 1906, the main railway arteries were used to move people and players from sporting venues across the country. Little sporting activity, as evidenced by the golf courses and racecourses of the time, took place far from the nearest station (photo: Irish Railway Records Society).

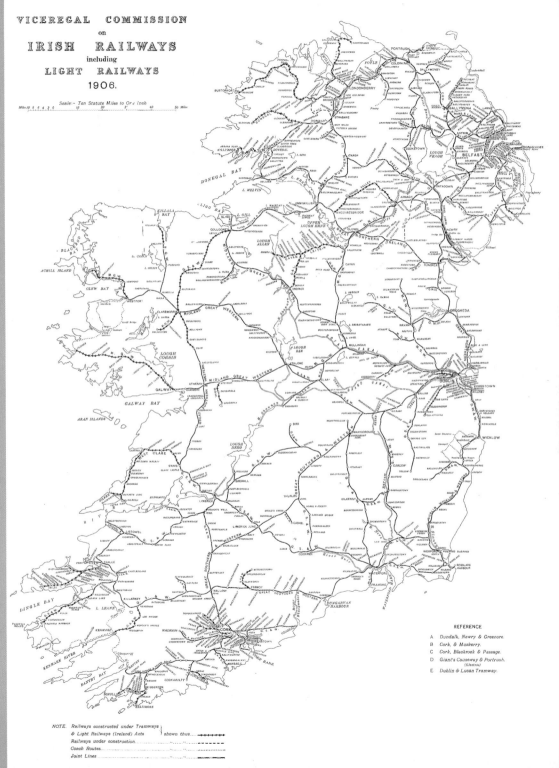

VICEREGAL COMMISSION
on
IRISH RAILWAYS
including
LIGHT RAILWAYS
1906.

Scale:- Ten Statute Miles to One Inch

REFERENCE

A   Dundalk, Newry & Greenore.
B   Cork, & Muskerry.
C   Cork, Blackrock & Passage.
D   Giant's Causeway & Portrush.
      (Electric)
E   Dublin & Lucan Tramway.

NOTE.   Railways constructed under Tramways
           & Light Railways (Ireland) Acts   } shown thus
           Railways under construction
           Coach Routes
           Joint Lines

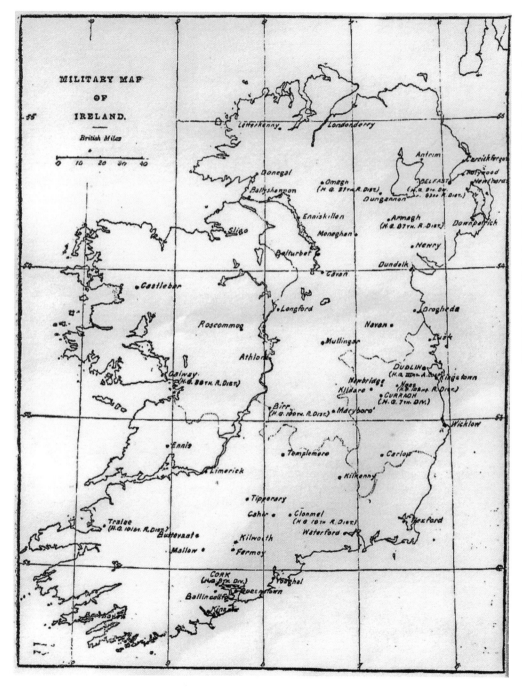

In the context of the cultural nationalism of the GAA, and the ban on 'foreign' sports, so-called garrison games were demonised. This was, in the late nineteenth century, an incredible act of historical revisionism, as the roots of many sporting clubs and sites across the country were the product of interaction between locals and the military stationed nearby. This map from 1903 demonstrates the scale of army garrisons across the island, but also mirrors the location of the major racing, golf, tennis, soccer, rugby and horse racing venues. The army was one of the key forces in the spread of sport across Ireland (photo: Irish Sporting Heritage).

The development of tourism in Ireland in the nineteenth century was a product of railways links, the belief that the outdoors and sea air were beneficial to the human body, and the access, for many workers, to vacation time. Towns such as Bray developed and prospered as a result, but in promoting themselves were always keen to highlight their sporting infrastructure (photo: Irish Sporting Heritage).

railway. While dependant on nature to produce rivers and lakes in which to fish, proximity to the railway meant that certain fishing locations were favoured over those at a greater distance from a station. In 1927, a guidebook produced by the Department of Lands and Fisheries, *The Angler's Guide to the Irish Free State*, listed all the main fishing areas in Ireland, with details of the types of fishing, where to stay and so on. One crucial piece of advice offered was the distance of the fishing venue from the nearest railway station. In an age before motorised private transport, the train was the key to accessing sport.

Railway companies understood their importance to the sporting public, and also the value of such business to their profits. As a result, the various railway companies were some of the first sponsors and supporters of sporting events. These included the Irish Railway Company's sponsorship of a cup for inter-county GAA from 1928, the Western Railway's decision to carry all competing racehorses to the Galway Races from 1864 and the myriad of discounted fares for supporters of most sports that were on offer from the 1870s and 1880s. Companies even formed their own sports clubs, such as Dundalk FC in County Louth, which, when it was formed in 1903, was originally known as Dundalk GNR (Great Northern Railway).

While the Irish railway network was severely truncated in the 1950s and 1960s, its sporting legacy is clear. Many of the major sporting towns on this island are those that were connected to the railway network at its peak. It is no accident that so many of the landmark golf clubs had a direct rail link, or that so many of the major racecourses had their own station. Equally, there was not one GAA county ground built that was not, at the time of construction, on a railway line.

Hand in hand with the spread of the railways was the evolution of Irish holiday towns. The same impulse that

Ireland has a proud record in the annals of boxing. One of its first heroes of the ring was Dan Donnelly, who defeated the Englishman Tom Hall in a fight at the Curragh in 1814. The fight was re-enacted, as shown here, in the 1950s, as part of the An Tóstal Festival. Then, as in 1814, crowds flocked to the natural amphitheatre to watch Jim Berney (acting as Donnelly) defeat his English opponent (photo: Irish Sporting Heritage).

drove the railway companies to service sporting venues encouraged them to extend their lines to those places where people wished to holiday. The second half of the nineteenth century, for certain groups of professional and manual workers, ushered in the idea of paid vacationing, and the railways extended their reach so that families could escape for their day out or their week's holiday. Towns such as Bray, Tramore, Salthill, Portrush and many others became the places to go, and be seen in, during the holiday season. To attract and then entertain tourists, many seaside towns invested in their sporting infrastructure. Sea bathing was a huge nineteenth-century attraction, as was the provision of purpose-built pools and lidos. Golf courses and tennis courses were built (either by town authorities or enterprising hoteliers) as a way of attracting more people, and various sporting events and spectacles, such as race meetings and athletics tournaments, were put on to draw a crowd. In the absence of wholesale investment in sports facilities provided from the public purse in urban areas, such seaside facilities also began to serve non-tourists from nearby conurbations that had no local provision. As travel and the nature of holidays changed, so did the ways in which sport was used to attract people to Ireland. During the late 1950s and into the 1960s, after it had opened its transatlantic routes, Aer Lingus regularly used Ireland's sporting attractions, particularly golf and fishing, in its advertising as a means of enticing Americans to Ireland for their holidays. Major events, such as the Irish Derby and the various Sweepstakes races, were a regular feature in the promotions undertaken abroad by the various predecessors of Fáilte Ireland. In addition to those participants that Irish tourism seeks to attract to the wealth of facilities such as golf courses and so on, recent major sporting spectacles such as the Special Olympics in 2003, the Ryder Cup in 2006 and the Europa Cup final in 2011 have been used to attract sporting tourists to Ireland. For all the natural beauty that Ireland has to offer, and the wealth of its history and literature, sport has always been present as a key driver of both internal and external tourism.

A large supporting role in the sporting revolution was played by the media. The growing number of newspapers, coupled with growing rates of literacy, in the second half of the nineteenth century changed the nature of communication in Ireland. The main newspapers had slowly developed an interest in sports coverage, beginning with horse racing, and it was no accident that Michael Cusack used the pages of the *United Irishmen* to publish his first rules of the GAA in January 1885. He understood the power of the press, and knew well that printed rules, which could be read across the length and breadth of the country, would lead to a degree of standardisation in the Association's games. The demand for sporting coverage led in 1881 to the opening of Ireland's first dedicated sporting newspaper, *Sport*. This title would run until the 1930s, and covered all the main sports of Ireland, offering a comprehensive results service, as well as match reports and colour pieces on the main athletes of the day. In a more upper class vein, but equally important, was the *Irish Field*, which concentrated, but not exclusively, on bloodstock-related matters at first, then developing its coverage to embrace rugby, soccer and cricket, and then later the new sports of motor car and motorcycling races. By the 1920s, the *Irish Times*, *Irish Independent* and *Cork Examiner* had all developed detailed sports pages, and when the *Irish Press* opened its doors in the 1930s, it excelled in its coverage of Gaelic games. In radio, the advent of 2RN (later Radio Éireann and RTÉ) in 1926 was not only a landmark event for the nation, but also for sport. In its pursuit of a range of Irish programming content, the station took the decision to offer live commentary of GAA matches, and in fact became the first station in Europe to offer live sports

The army played a key role in the development of modern sport as they moved around Ireland. This camp at the Curragh in the 1890s demonstrates the size and scale of the army on the move, but also hints at the necessary temporary accommodation before buildings were erected. As the building of the Curragh gained momentum, a range of sporting facilities followed to ensure that the soldiers were occupied during their leisure time (photo: National Library of Ireland).

Many sporting bodies claim to have been first in creating an organisation, a sport and a set of rules. In Ireland, the most significant early starter was the Irish Turf Club. The governing authority for horse racing to this day, the Club was founded in 1790, and is currently housed in these offices at the Curragh (photo: Damien Murphy).

Left: Some sports evolve, and others are invented. The GAA, under the guidance of Michael Cusack, can be considered an invention as a means of resisting the dominance of British sporting culture. In such incidences, the place of origin takes on a huge significance, and the site becomes one of heritage. Here, Ireland's most notable sporting birthplace, Hayes Hotel, in Thurles, continues doing business as it did in November 1884 when Cusack brought his small but revolutionary band together (photo: Damien Murphy).

coverage. This was followed in 1961 with the start-up of Irish television, and here again RTÉ quickly developed a reputation for its screening of GAA, soccer, rugby and horse racing, amongst others. The role of the media in popularising sport was central to the success of various sports taking a hold on people's leisure time. It brought people together, who may not have been able to attend a match or fixture, and allowed them to buy into the events of the day. This resulted in a shared sporting awareness across the country, and at the level of the local media, an embrace of community-based sports.

While the media had little impact per se on the built sporting environment (beyond the need for stadia to include space for journalists, commentators and camera crews), it was important for the public awareness of sporting sites. The words of Paddy Mehigan or the voices of Micheál O'Hehir at Croke Park or Philip Greene at Dalymount were critical in connecting sports followers with place. To read a report, to listen to a commentary or to watch a match on television allowed a multitude of the population to become part of the event. Through the media they connected with events on the pitch, but also began to identify the day with the stadium where a match was taking place. So, even if a GAA fan has never travelled to Croke Park or a rugby fan to the Aviva Stadium, they know through the media that these grounds are iconic and a central strand in their appreciation of sport. The nation's listeners and viewers understand the value and significance of the stage on which matches are played.

Although a complex relationship, the British army's impact on Ireland is undeniable. It was a long-standing presence and one which, by the time the last British troops left the Free State in 1922, had left an indelible mark on the Irish sporting landscape. There are two central issues to consider here: the sheer number of British troops who passed through Ireland in the nineteenth and early twentieth centuries, and the geographical spread of their operations. The thousands of soldiers based in Ireland, as elsewhere in the world, needed to fill their leisure time. The British army was central to the spread of sport across the world as it believed in the value of sport in entertaining and occupying its men, and the benefits that could be accrued for garrison-town relations by playing with the locals. In Ireland, garrisons grew up alongside the railway network and made a significant contribution to their local setting. Not only did they provide work for locals and a boost to the local economy through their spending power, but they also provided the genesis for a host of sporting clubs and support for a variety of sporting events. The imprint of the military can be seen in their involvement in the foundation of a multitude of golf clubs, race courses, tennis clubs, soccer clubs and rugby clubs. Soldiers in the British Army had the knowledge of sport, the time (and often resources) and the local connections to make things happen. The power of the army connection is clear when considering the early years of golf in Ireland: of the first twelve golf clubs founded in Ireland, only the Island Golf Club (founded 1890) in Donabate, County Dublin, was brought to life without the involvement of army personnel. Clearly the advent of the GAA, which specifically excluded members of the army, and the deteriorating conditions in the country in the late nineteenth century, led the army to retreat from the field and into barracks, but their role in building the sporting infrastructure of Ireland is perhaps their most positive legacy.

The final piece of the infrastructure jigsaw that enabled sport to develop in Ireland were those administrators and associations which ran Irish sport. The power of the governing body in the development of sport was central to the success of the whole enterprise. Without standard rules, a body to enforce discipline and organise competitions, sport would have remained an ad hoc, and perhaps

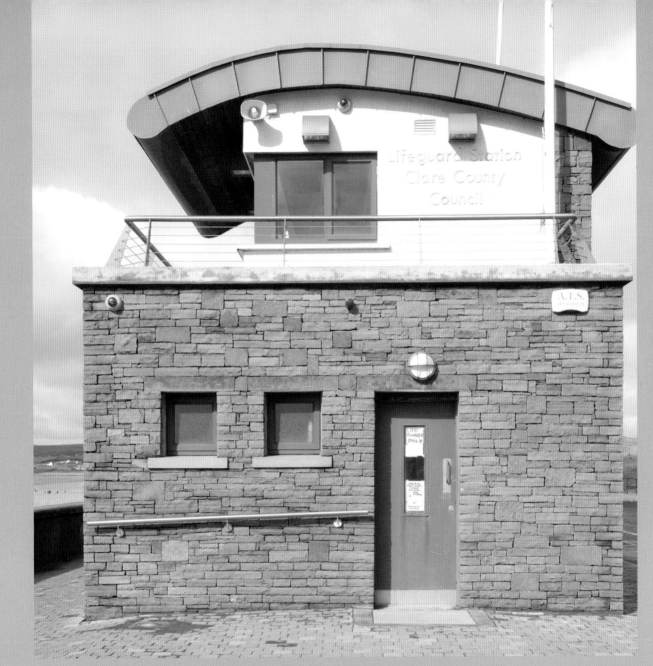

Above and facing page: Surfing in Ireland probably began in the 1940s, with Joe Roddy launching his home-made board into the waves off Dundalk, County Louth. The west of Ireland has, in recent years, become a Mecca for surfers looking to ride the Atlantic swells. For a sport which prides itself on its affinity with nature and the open sea, the participants still have created around them a built sporting heritage. Here at Lahinch, while surfers take to the waves, they are watched over by those manning the adjacent lifeguard station, built by the local council (pictures: Damien Murphy).

unsuccessful, enterprise. Once national bodies were founded, clubs around the country affiliated and leagues and cup competitions flourished. When a governing body lost its way, as with the GAA after the Parnell split in 1890, and the ensuing battle for control between the Irish Republican Brotherhood and the Catholic Church, the effect on sport was devastating. In the 1890s, the GAA lost thousands of members, clubs folded and the Association itself came close to extinction. The GAA recovered, but the effect of the split in athletics between the Irish Amateur Athletics Association and the National Athletics and Cycling Association in the 1930s was devastating and one could argue that this protracted dispute, more than anything else, hampered the successful development of athletics in Ireland.

In terms of the built environment for sport, governing bodies have played an important role. They have lobbied government for funds, and once these were secured, they spent them across the country developing grounds and pitches. This was most impressively done by Padraig O'Caoimh in the GAA during the 1930s and 1940s, who oversaw the Association's purchase and development of most of its key county grounds. The power of governing bodies as lobbyists, if nothing else, has been clear in recent decades. With the advent of the National Lottery in 1987 and the distribution of the proceeds in terms of grants by the government department controlling sport, governing bodies have been highly vocal in lobbying for the development of sporting infrastructure. In 2010, €48 million was disbursed by government in the Irish Republic to assist the ongoing development of sporting sites and equipment provision under the terms of the Sports Capital Programme. In 2008, for example, the monies that were granted covered a range of sports across the country, including the Gorey Community Badminton Centre, Mullingar Jets Swim Club, Banagher United Soccer Club, Ballivor Clay Pigeon Shooting Club and Galway Kayak Club.

The infrastructure that helped to develop, and has since supported, sport, is wide ranging. Without the military, the railways or the media, sport would not have developed in the way that it did. And neither would the built sporting environment. All these different elements acted as agencies for the development of sporting sites, in specific places, for a variety of reasons. As the infrastructure dictated where sport would be played and ensured its popularity in any given location, so the process of building venues began.

6

INSTITUTIONS

IN ADDITION to the infrastructure that supported and promoted the diffusion of sport, there was a key set of institutions in Irish life which believed that sport and physical exercise would benefit their communities. As such, these institutions invested in sport and, in part, helped create Ireland's sporting environment. These institutions usually viewed sport as something that was morally and physically beneficial, and can be seen as acting in a philanthropic or altruistic manner in their approach to supporting sporting activity.

One of the most powerful forces in late-nineteenth-century Ireland was the Catholic Church. In line with many other denominations across Europe, it was a keen advocate of sport as it recognised the moral value of the new codified forms, with their built-in appeals to gentlemanly conduct and fair play. Church support was significant in the Irish context, as the Catholic hierarchy, as distinct from their Protestant brethren, had no problem with the question of Sunday play. This was vital for the GAA in its early years, and the link between the Church and the Association was important in establishing Gaelic games as central to Irish life. The Church, through its control of much of the schooling system, was a keen advocate of sport for young men and women, and most schools featured some form of physical exercise on their curriculum. The choice of sport within any given school often came down to the interests of principals, individual

priests or the favoured sport of any given order. Alongside its presence in schools, the Church's most important step in terms of institutionalising sport came through its lay organisation, the Catholic Young Men's Society (CYMS), which was established in 1849.

The CYMS grew steadily in the nineteenth century and later received a boost when it was part of a wider movement in the 1930s, seeking to promote Catholic social action. It took its model in part from the YMCA, which had been founded in London in 1844. The CYMS spread rapidly and one its main attractions was the range of sports and facilities it offered to its members. The work of Michael O'Rourke on the history of Wexford CYMS is indicative of the range of events that the Society supported. The great Wexford football team of the 1914–18 period used the CYMS gymnasium to train, Jem Roche, who fought for the world heavyweight title in 1908 trained there, the club produced national champions in motor cycling, as well as county champions in table tennis, cycling, snooker and billiards and, as recently as 1999, club member Rodney Goggins won the world under-21 amateur snooker championship. The CYMS still has clubs across Ireland and it has been an important institution (certainly through to the 1950s when numbers began declining) in offering a sporting outlet to Catholic men.

Most people have their first taste of organised sport in school. The whole area of schooling, and in particular

In the diffusion of sport across Ireland, educational institutions, particularly schools, have been key. The placing of sport on the curriculum from the 1870s, as a means of inculcating good spirit within boys, meant that sport became part of their lives. The religious played a central role in promoting sport in Irish schools and in deciding which games were played. Here, at Clongowes Wood in 1903, the Jesuit staff demonstrate their love of cricket, a game that was later played by James Joyce when he attended the school (picture: Irish Jesuit Archives).

denominational control, was a constant source of debate in the nineteenth century. In most of that century, in addition to well-established Church of Ireland schools across the country, there was a network of private academies that educated those children whose families could afford the fees, as well as schools run by the Christian Brothers and other orders. The standard provision of schooling to all children began in earnest with the 1831 Education Act, and later cemented by the 1873 Irish Education Bill. The National School system spread to cover the country, and a process of building an ever wider network of schools was continued after independence. In all this, the fortunes of sport were mixed. While some elite schools around the country built lavish sporting facilities for their pupils, such as Blackrock College (founded 1860), Clongowes Wood (1814), the Royal School in Armagh (1608), Midleton College in Cork (1609), St Colman's College in Newry (1823) and St Columb's in Derry (1879), many schools had little or no sports provision.

While the majority of schools now offer a wide range of sporting choices for their pupils, they are often traditionally associated with a particular code, whether rugby or GAA. For girls, traditions have also been built around certain sports, such as hockey at Wesley College, Dublin, and camogie at St Raphael's, Gort, or St Mary's Secondary, Charleville. Whatever sporting facilities now serve a school, the development of such was often piecemeal. Wesley College, for example, began life on St Stephen's Green, Dublin, in 1845, but originally had no sports grounds of its own. In common with many schools, it used local facilities and open spaces on which to play. The sporting ethos of the school was clear, as its old boys established the Old Wesley rugby club in 1879, and the school was a founder member of the Leinster Schools Cup. As the school grew, and became spread across various city centre sites, so places such as the grounds of the Royal

Hospital Donnybrook were used for sport and a boys' pavilion constructed. By the late 1940s, a new sports pavilion and pitches were laid out for the school in Bloomfield. In 1969, the school relocated to its current site at Ballinteer where there are the necessary facilities for rugby, cricket, hockey, netball, athletics, tennis and other sports.

Beyond the fee-paying schools with long histories, and the necessary space for multiple facilities, most schools in Ireland have provided, since the introduction of mandatory physical education in the 1930s, what is legally required of them. Depending on the setting of the school, and the space which it has available, this can stretch from using a playground or indoor gymnasium, all the way through to multiple outdoor, all-weather and floodlit pitches. So, while the facilities on offer have historically varied widely, and still vary today, schools have been an important supplier of sporting sites and facilities across the country.

The original homes of many sports in Ireland were in its universities. The oldest clubs at Trinity College for example, are the cricket club (1835), boat club (1836), football club (1854) and soccer club (1883). The presence of these clubs within the University, and the authority's encouragement of student sports led to the building of the pitches and pavilions in the College, and the University boathouse on the Liffey. Trinity now boasts fifty sports for its student body, a number equalled by the National University of Ireland colleges. Many of the sports that were taken up by students came to life as a result of varsity competition, such as the Fitzgibbon Cup in hurling, which started in 1912. Originally contested by Cork, Galway and UCD, the competition now encompasses all third level colleges. University sport, which has always been driven by the enthusiasm and sporting tastes of the students, has received critical support from the institutions. While initial pitches and playing facilities may have been provided by

While many sports have over the decades entered the public sphere in terms of ground location, city or state ownership and spectator demands, many others exist in private settings. For example, Mullingar Cricket Club has, since the 1970s, played on a pitch in the grounds of Mount Murray in Bunbrosna, which was offered to them by the Murray family who have a deep love of the game (photo: Irish Sporting Heritage).

Patronage was of paramount importance in the emergence of many sporting sites. Newbrook Racecourse in Mullingar was chaired and supported by Lord Greville, the MP for Westmeath from 1865 to 1874. The racecourse opened in 1852, had its own railway station, and stayed in business until 1961 (picture: Westmeath Library Service).

The Defence Forces were founded in 1922 with the creation of an independent Irish State. A key part of the military experience across the world has been the promotion of sport as part of what soldiers do. The Defence Forces promote nineteen different sports amongst their ranks, and their various sporting facilities include their pitches and pavilion in Phoenix Park (picture: Damien Murphy).

Left: Swimming indoors was not something that many Irish people got to experience until well into the twentieth century. The oldest existing indoor swimming pool in Ireland was built in 1904 for the seminarians of St Patrick's College, Maynooth. It survives to this day as the campus pool for NUI Maynooth (photo: Irish Sporting Heritage).

The Iveagh Trust was established by Sir Edward Guinness, to assist the poor of Dublin. The Trust's largest undertaking was a series of Iveagh Trust buildings, constructed from 1901, between Bull Alley and Bride Road in Dublin. At the heart of the buildings lay the Iveagh Trust Public Baths, built to provide people in the neighbourhood with somewhere to wash and swim. The Baths were designed by Joseph & Smithem, and the building works supervised by Kaye Parry & Ross. The Baths were formally opened on 6 June 1906. In recent years the Baths have been renovated and now function as a multi-purpose contemporary fitness centre (photo: Irish Sporting Heritage).

Carlow Mental Hospital Sports

IN AID OF THE CHAPELS' FUND,
THURSDAY, 15th JUNE, 1922.

President—DR. GREENE.
Vice-President—DR. McKENNA.

Judges—Rev. Canon Ridgeway, Rev. J. Killian, Adm.; Rev. J. C. Nelson, W. P. Hade, Esq., C.E.

Lap-Keepers—P. Coyne, J. Foley, J. Kinsella, W. Hayden.

Timekeeper—G. Douglas, senr.

Umpires—Rev. Bro. Keegan, J. Foley, A. Greene.

Stewards—T. Ryan, G. Douglas, junr.; W. Mulhall, M. Kirwan, E. Doogue, G. Brennan, S. Nolan, P. Doyle, J. Butler, J. Foley, etc.

Hon. Secs.—A. Greene, W. Hayden.

ORDER OF EVENTS.

1. 100 Yards. Confined.
2. 1 Mile Cycle. Confined.
3. Long Jump. Confined.
4. 28lbs. from Circle. Confined
5. 100 Yards. Open.
6. 1 Mile Cycle. Open.
7. 220 Yards. Championship of Carlow.
8. 3 Mile Cycle. Confined.
9. 440 Yards. Open.
10. 4 Miles. Championship of Leinster.
11. Long Jump. Open.
12. Ladies' Cycle. Open.
13. 2 Miles Cycle. Confined.
14. 880 Yards. Open.
15. High Jump.
16. 2 Miles Cycle Championship of Carlow.
17. 100 Yards. Ladies
18. 56lbs. for Height.
19. 3 Miles Cycle. Open.
20. 440 Yards. Confined.
21. 100 Yards. Veterans.
22. Composite Race.
23. 1 Mile Flat. Open.
24. 5 Miles Cycle. Open.
25. Patients' Race.
26. 880 Yards. Confined.
27. Siamese Race.
28. Tilting the Bucket.

EVENT 1.   100 YARDS. CONFINED.

First Prize—Irish Rug, Presented by M. Molloy, Esq. Second—Case of Tea Knives.

J. Kinsella
M. Neill.
W. Hayden.
M. Lawler.
W. Neill.
P. Brien

W. Kelly.
P. Norris.
J. Carroll.
W. Jones.
R. Jordan.
C. Souhan.

Won by   2nd,   3rd,

EVENT 2.   ONE MILE CYCLE. CONFINED.

First Prize—Cruet Stand.   Second Prize—Wedgewood Butter Dish.

W. Hayden.
M. Neill.
M. Lawler.
P. Brien
P. Power.

J. Kinsella.
P. Norris.
R. Jordan.
C. Souhan.
W. Jones.

Won by   2nd,   3rd,

The Community Games were established in Dublin in 1968 as a means of tackling the lack of sporting and leisure provision for youngsters in urban settings. Now a national organisation, it encompasses over 50,000 competitors. Here, the children from Edenmore parade through the centre of Dublin in 1976 (picture: Dublin City Libraries).

the university for altruistic reasons, more recently the provision of top-quality facilities has been seen as a given if institutions wish to attract students. This has been evidenced by the number of new facilities built in recent years (such as the €22 million sports centre built by NUI Galway and completed in 2009 or the University of Limerick's state-of-the-art sports arena), and the way in which newer entrants into the ranks of third level colleges, such as Dublin City University, have invested heavily in a

sporting infrastructure and student bursaries, as a way of attracting high levels of applicants and, amongst them, some of the best student athletes in the country. Then, as now, graduating students are critical for the spread and support of various sports once they leave college.

One of the many institutions that have supported sport since the nineteenth century has been the workplace. Many teams across Ireland, such as Cork Constitution, originally a cricket and later a rugby team (established 1892), drew its members from the staff of the newspaper bearing the same name. Such a drawing together of workers so that they could play and socialise together was common practice at the end of the nineteenth century and into the twentieth, and bodies such as the Civil Service Cricket Club (1863), the Railway Union Sports Club (1904), and the Defence Forces Athletic Association (1924) all emerged from within the workplace. Through support from their employers, or else through fund-raising and the collection of subscriptions, many of these clubs have been able to purchase or lease their own grounds and build facilities.

Some employers were particularly enlightened in terms of providing sports facilities and played a key role in promoting sport in Ireland. The most recognisable of these is Guinness, which established the Guinness Athletic Union (GAU) as a means of encouraging the brewery's employees to take part in sport. Based at the Iveagh grounds, the GAU also gave life to teams that played at the elite level, such as St James's Gate FC (founded in 1902), a founder member of the League of Ireland in 1921 and inaugural winner of the FAI Cup. Other large private, state and semi-state companies that followed Guinness in providing a full range of facilities for its workers include Aer Lingus, the ESB and Bank of Ireland. Many of these workplace sporting clubs operate around the country, and as a result sporting facilities were erected to serve various sports and the workers wishing to play in most counties.

The final institution to support the development of sport in its early days, and which had the necessary funds to build some of Ireland's first sporting structures, was the 'big house'. Many of the sports that were played by the residents of such houses were for their own, and their friends', enjoyment. These were often traditional sports associated with country estates, such as shooting and fishing. Equestrian sports were also important, and the desire to ride and race led many owners of big houses either to open their own grounds to racing or, as with the Locke family in Westmeath, provide a field for racing to take place (this was in 1879, and became the Kilbeggan Races). Team games, most notably cricket, were also sponsored by landlords, and the Marquess of Ormonde in Kilkenny and the Parnells in Wicklow were early supporters of the game. The first recorded game in Kilkenny was played at Kilkenny Castle in 1829, and by 1839 it had become such a fixture that the Ordnance Survey map shows the cricket ground there. Through to the middle of the nineteenth century, cricket in Kilkenny, for example, as Michael O'Dwyer has shown, was regularly played on the big estates of Gowran Castle, Castlecomer, Foulkscourt, Bessborough, and Desart Court near Callan. With the advent of the Land War, and the ever-widening gap in the relationship between the occupier of the big house and those around them, sports that could be played exclusively amongst fellow-minded people of the same class became more common. Here, it was the private club games of tennis, or else involvement in the growing number of golf clubs in the later decades of the nineteenth century, that gave the big house occupiers a means to play. While many of these estates are now derelict or have disappeared, it is not physically obvious what sport was played there. It is, however, clear from the society pages of the newspapers that the big house, in the form of hosting and taking part in sport, was a key institution in its nineteenth-century development.

These institutions all played an important role in making sport happen and, in their different ways and with varying levels of access to land and wealth, put in place much of Ireland's sporting built environment. Combined with the infrastructure, discussed in the previous chapter, institutions were central in spreading the gospel of sport across Ireland.

7
SPORTING PLACES

Sporting places vary greatly. While we are often drawn to think of major stadia, most of us first experience sport as play, in a local setting. Such games are often spontaneous rather than organised, and adapt play to the space available. In urban spaces this is especially apparent, as games are often played out in tight spaces, such as this game of rounders in Pearse Square in the 1970s, taking place beside a gable end (photo: Dublin City Libraries).

S PORT IS, as we have argued, centrally important to Irish life. It operates broadly in two ways: first, as a spectacle and, second, as a participatory activity. What both the top player who is watched by his or her fans and the club sportsperson have in common is that they require facilities to play their games. The scale may differ but in both cases history – and often nature – has dictated where those facilities are and what form they take.

Since the second half of the nineteenth century, sport has made a visible impact on the Irish landscape. It has

Many sporting events do not require permanent facilities as they take place only on a once-off or infrequent basis. In the 1920s, Phoenix Park began hosting motor races and in 1929 was the setting for the Irish International Motor Race, or Grand Prix as we would understand it now. The event was heavily backed by the government of the time, and crowds in excess of 100,000 attended. Around the course, various temporary stands were constructed to ensure that the VIPs could watch in comfort (photo: National Library of Ireland).

Horse racing is a sport that requires large spaces and, as a result, many of the first courses were rurally based but made accessible by the advent of the railways. One of the oldest courses in Ireland is Bellewstown, County Meath, which held its first recorded race in 1726 and also included, inside the track, a cricket ground (photo: Bellewstown Racecourse).

Golf has a long history in Ireland, and most early courses worked with the coastal landscape. The famous Ballybunnion course was constructed by members of the Black Watch and Prince of Charles Regiment, who were holidaying in the area. Work on the course began in 1893, but such was the piecemeal development of golf courses at the time that Ballybunnion did not become a full eighteen-hole course until 1927. The challenges and beauty of the course are a product of its location on the Kerry coast, and it is regularly listed as one of the finest golf clubs in the world (photo: Irish Sporting Heritage).

Bray Wanderers came into being in 1922, following a dispute in the ranks of the St Kevin's GAA club. The current home of Bray, the Carlisle Grounds, predates the soccer club, having opened in 1862 as the Bray Athletic Ground. The ground was designed by William Dargan, and served as a multi-sport venue. In the 1910s and 1920s, it became associated with soccer when the Bray Unknowns began playing there, and they were followed into the ground by the Wanderers (photos: Irish Sporting Heritage).

entertained countless spectators, has provided contests and physical challenges to its participants, and has acted both as an instrument of cohesion and division in society. Sport has had a significant impact on the economy. This is not simply a matter of gate receipts from the top sports, but also revenue derived from the making and selling of sports equipment, employment and contracts derived from the construction and upkeep of sporting facilities, and the income produced by tourists visiting Ireland for sport, notably golf, equestrian sports and fishing. All of these economic factors heightened the impact that sport had on the landscape. It was not simply a matter of a ground or course being built, but, as we have noted, the infrastructure that was wrapped around it: transport routes that were built to afford easy access to sporting sites, changing rooms and clubhouses that were built to cater for players and spectators, hotels that arose to cater for sporting tourists and restaurants and bars that grew up around major venues.

The first sporting facilities of the nineteenth century were usually temporary affairs. Field sports such as football, hurling or rugby were often played on borrowed land, and markings laid out just for the match. Similarly, horse racing and golf, although adapting to and using the natural contours of the landscape, did not develop fixed and maintained sites until the later nineteenth century. For example, Royal Belfast Golf Club, the oldest in Ireland, started playing in 1881 on land owned by the Laird of Holywood, which he provided rent free. However, the club left that site at Kinnegar, Holywood, and moved to a new nine-hole course at Carnalea, Bangor in 1892. It was not until 1925, when the club bought Craigavad House and its grounds, that it became permanently housed on its own premises. In common with many early clubs, across a variety of sports, moves from one site to another were often the way of a club's initial decades as they sought a permanent home that was fit for purpose.

Land ownership has always been a contentious issue in Ireland, and the access to fields and spaces for sport, was difficult. While sports such as cricket, golf, tennis and horse racing could rely either on land being granted to them by enthusiastic members, or else those who had the means to club together and buy land, for many sports patronised by the working classes, access to permanent sites was often beyond their means.

Many GAA clubs were not able to buy their own pitches until after the Second World War, while the sports of soccer and rugby, often had to rely on local patronage to secure their playing surfaces. The Dundalk Young Irelands GAA club, which can claim to be one of the oldest in the country, won the inaugural Louth championship in 1887. The venue was borrowed, and played in what was described as 'McGeough's Field'. The tenuous nature of a 'home' venue is clear in the Young Irelands story. After moving between pitches on borrowed lands, the club settled in at the town's Athletic Grounds, until these were closed in 1959. From then, the club relied on land lent to it by the Marist Brothers until 1989. After that, and a huge amount of fund-raising, the club was finally able, after a century in existence, to move into a property that it owned, Pairc Eire Óg, where it remains to this day.

Despite the uncertainties facing clubs such as Young Irelands, at least many team sports could, so long as the potential pitch was accessible and flat, go anywhere in the locality that was offered to them. Their spatial requirements were quite limited. The same was true of other sports, often based around the private club, such as tennis, bowls and croquet, but these were more likely, due to the demographic of their memberships, to be able to purchase their own sites. Rushbrooke Lawn Tennis and Croquet Club, in Cobh, County Cork, is the oldest existing croquet club in Ireland, having been founded in 1882 (although the game is recorded as having been played there from 1870). The club was able to secure lands precisely because of those for whom it catered: British military officers and the local professional classes. The commitment of the membership and its financial ability is evident in the fact that, by 1887, a club pavilion had been built to cater for the players. For sports such as golf, especially when in its early years the seaside links course reigned supreme, the land required was sizeable and the work necessary to make it fit for play was a considerable undertaking and needed years of development to complete. As with all sporting surfaces, golf courses require constant upkeep and are regularly extended or upgraded. St Anne's Golf Club on North Bull Island, Dublin, opened its doors

in 1921, but in 2003 a major redevelopment of the course and clubhouse began, with five tees and eight greens being replaced. Much of the work was completed with turf that had been removed from Croke Park during its own rebuilding process.

As the case studies in this book will show, it was the enclosure of sporting facilities that fundamentally altered the Irish landscape, and produced the sporting heritage that we are concerned with. Once grounds, pitches and courses became owned by those who patronised them, so the issue of controlling access became key. For commercial undertakings, which wanted to charge admission, entrance gates and turnstiles had to be built to allow those who paid to enter, while walls and fences were constructed to keep out those who could not pay. Fraher Field, in Dungarvan, was initially leased for sporting purposes in 1885. Prior to the construction of permanent structures on the site in the 1910s, access to the grounds was controlled by rudimentary fencing, and the playing surface simply roped off from supporters. Such basic crowd control, and the lack of actual facilities for spectators, would have been entirely normal in the late nineteenth and early twentieth centuries. For private clubs, whose members paid an annual or once-off fee to access the facility, perimeters were built up to ensure the exclusive access to the sport that members wanted. At one level this was simply about security and privacy, but it was also about social control. Be it through a membership application process or by the charges made,

The majority of GAA clubs around Ireland serve small communities. Given the Association's volunteer, community and amateur ethos, it has been able to distribute its profits so that even the smallest club has been able to develop modern facilities. Here in Cushendall, Antrim, the floodlit pitches and clubhouse, nestled under the shadow of Lurigethan Mountain are a far cry from the basic field that would have been used by the club when it was founded in the 1920s by Father George McKillop (photo: Peter Higgins).

One of the great natural challenges in the calendar of Irish sport is the annual Poc Fada championship. It began life in 1961 and is held every summer. The 5km course crosses Annaverna Mountain in County Louth and combines the skill of the modern hurler with the legends of Cúchulainn. Shown here, the 2009 champion, Gerry Fallon from Roscommon, sets out to defend his title a year later against the stunning natural backdrop (photo: Shay Larkin www.anpocfada.net).

private sport clubs explicitly included, and excluded, people. Omagh Tennis Club was founded in 1892 on Crevenagh Road, where it remains. It serviced the professional and military classes of the town. A sense of the club's social exclusivity, like many tennis clubs across the country, is evidenced in a pre-First World War ritual: the Saturday Tea Day. Each week a lady member would act as hostess and provide tea for any members and their invited guests who cared to attend. To enter the gates of the club and take part in this weekly ritual was contingent on membership, and those not approved for entry were excluded.

With the raising of revenue, either from gate receipts or membership fees, sporting venues developed beyond the pitch or course. Depending on the financial circumstances of any given club, so buildings sprang up around the field of play. At the most basic and rudimentary level, the usual first step – the initial building – was a changing room or pavilion. For commercial sports, the need to cater for spectators was paramount. No matter what the attraction of the sport, those who paid into the ground needed to see the action. Terraces were built to allow people to stand and see the game more clearly, and later came stands that catered for those who wanted to sit and enjoy the match. The better the facilities on offer, such as a seat in a covered stand, the higher the price that could be charged and greater revenue produced. At Lansdowne Road, for example, which began life as an athletics ground in 1872, the first stand to house paying rugby spectators was not constructed until 1908. At Leopardstown Racecourse, which had opened in 1888, facilities grew up quickly such was the popularity amongst all classes for racing. The lines of separation between classes at Leopardstown, once they had paid their entrance fee, were clear as early as 1902. By that point, general admission was three shillings, but a member, on paying an annual fee of five guineas, could enter the members' enclosure with two female guests, go to a separate area in the paddock, and also avail of a parking space (the presumption being, even in those early days of motoring, that such members had a car rather than a carriage).

The building of such spectator facilities was a huge financial undertaking, and often a risk. If the expected crowds did not come, financial troubles and closure were the result. Sports that have struggled to keep the necessary spectator numbers, such as speedway, have seen facilities close or else the sport disappear altogether from the Irish landscape. Also, as the needs of spectators are not static and their expectations have changed over time, there has been a need for constant updating. The recent changes to Thomond Park, for example, have been driven by the desire of supporters to enjoy their games in modern, comfortable and well-serviced grounds. Health and safety concerns have also been an issue. Having large crowds in one place is a potentially dangerous situation. Given the experience of English soccer in the 1980s and 1990s, and the lessons learnt from the loss of life at Hillsborough and Bradford, major sporting bodies in Ireland were alerted to the problems posed by outdated stadia, wooden stands and crowd control. The fear of a major incident at key end-of-season matches was a significant factor in convincing the GAA to rebuild Croke Park in the 1990s.

While the scale of facilities available to spectators, from corporate boxes to bars and restaurants, may have changed over the years, the central concern for the organisers has been to get as many people through the gate as possible, and to have those spectators spend as much money as they can while in the ground.

An event such as an All-Ireland final or a rugby international has to be staged in a setting where 50–80,000 people all have a clear view of the game, and where they can enter, congregate and exit safely. The demands of these

All sporting sites develop and change with the passing of the years. Semple Stadium, a regular home of the Munster hurling finals, began life as the Thurles sportsfield at the beginning of the twentieth century. Initially leased to the GAA, the ground was formally taken over by the Association in 1956. A major rebuilding programme was undertaken in the 1930s so that the golden jubilee hurling final could be played there in front of 60,000 spectators. The ground was redeveloped again in the 1960s, and has recently been modernised once more (photo: Damien Murphy).

What is striking about modern stadia designed for elite sports and large numbers of spectators, is their sheer size. Here the recently rebuilt Thomond Park dwarfs every other building in Limerick, and physically demonstrates how central the game of rugby has been to the history and development of the city (photo: Munsterimages.ie).

large crowds have controlled the design of sporting spaces. Stands were built in the relevant contemporary style and materials: first with wood, concrete (the first reinforced concrete stands in Ireland, designed by Donnelly, Moore, Keefe and Robinson, were built at Baldoyle Racecourse in 1919 and Lansdowne Road, by Donnelly, Moore and Keatinge in 1926: both have since been demolished) and then steel. Where the first stands were simply about affording a better view, in time issues of comfort, such as keeping patrons covered from the elements, social elitism and exclusion, and later the demands for bars, restaurants and conference facilities beneath the stands, have all dictated what has been built.

Across Ireland however, the majority of sporting spaces are not concerned with large-scale crowds. Most sporting spaces are there for the use of the local community, the parish or for the members of the private club. While books have to balance, the impetus behind these sporting spaces, those at local level, are not driven by the need to cater for mass spectators or to maximise commercial profits. As a result, the local GAA, cricket, tennis or bowling club is concerned with providing a service – a place to play – for those in the locality. There may be major matches in the year that draw a crowd, but essentially the facilities are for those that play. Here, the needs of the player – somewhere to change, store equipment, and maybe to socialise – are paramount. In these sporting spaces, the buildings around the ground may be limited to simple utilitarian structures. In clubs where staff were employed, such as groundskeepers or professionals, huts, sheds and shops were also built. These were usually the most basic of structures, and strict rules of social separation were enforced. Eddie Hackett, who was head professional at Portmarnock from 1939–50, while allowed to teach the members, was not allowed into the clubhouse.

But what then is Ireland's sporting heritage? As argued in the next chapter, the range and depth of buildings, stands, structures and courses that exist in Ireland (and which have disappeared) are a fascinating mix. There are golf courses that were built over a century ago, and which were adapted to work with the landscape. There are clubhouses and pavilions in private clubs, schools and colleges that are architecturally significant and opulent, given their sporting usage. There are changing rooms and storage buildings for equipment that were constructed cheaply, using voluntary labour, to serve their purpose, but have no aesthetic or architectural value. It is a complex mix of buildings that speaks of the history of Ireland. This sporting heritage tells the historic story, not simply of sport, but of social elites, colonial connections, national resistance, mass entertainment, and commercialisation. It charts economic upturns and downturns, reflects fashions in leisure and tourism, tells stories of patronage, announces trends in architectural design and building technology. It speaks of crowds and gatherings, of public order and disorder, rational recreation and folkloric pastimes. It illustrates how, even at the level of recreation, the ownership and development of land and property in Ireland has been a key issue in Irish history. It is a sporting landscape which has been governed and dictated largely, in comparison with other western nations, by clubs, organisations and associations, rather than by the state or the municipality.

8

SPORTING HERITAGE

WHAT MAKES A SPORTING SITE a place of heritage? This is a taxing question, as sporting sites in some ways are different from many other buildings and places that are seen as important parts of Ireland's heritage. One of the key issues in sports geography, and one which dominated debate in Britain in the 1980s and 1990s, is the question of topophilia, that is, a love of place. Against the backdrop of many professional soccer clubs moving from grounds they had occupied for decades, many supporters' groups argued vociferously that such a move betrayed the history of the club. Scholars argued that here, many sports fans were demonstrating their topophilia. So while some clubs have moved grounds, others such as Manchester United or Newcastle United have stayed put. The supporters love Old Trafford or St James' Park respectively and a move away seems an unfathomable option. But simply because sports players and supporters may love their sporting site, their 'home', does it mean that it is a place of heritage? Clearly, a site such as Old Trafford has an incredible historical significance in the game of soccer and to the people of Manchester, but as the physical nature of the ground has changed in light of commercial and health and safety requirements, what stands there now has no architectural

or physical relationship to what was there in the past. As such, Old Trafford could be considered a site of sporting heritage, but there is nothing physical there now that, of itself, is important. The same would be true of Croke Park or Lansdowne Road/Aviva Stadium. While places of great sporting, and in the context of Croke Park political, significance, there is nothing on the existing sites that pre-dates their respective redevelopments that began in the 1990s. So, important heritage places, yes, but significant heritage structures, no. And herein lies one of the problems for sporting sites: they are constantly evolving and, while they may be much loved, their existent heritage potential is unclear.

For most heritage sites in Ireland and elsewhere, the two major considerations relate to history and landscape, or effectively, what is being preserved. The aim in identifying Kilmainham Gaol as a heritage site, for example, is to preserve it. Walking through the Gaol on a tour, one is looking at a site as it was when Parnell, Pearse or de Valera were imprisoned there. The same is true, to a degree, of areas of natural heritage, such as the Burren. The agenda for the carers of that site is to preserve its natural beauty, to control access and development, and to ensure that its unique flora, fauna and geography can thrive

In May 2008, the Volvo Ocean Race stopped in Galway for a week. Hugely popular with the locals, tourists and sailing enthusiasts, the event created a new spectacle in Galway's rich sporting heritage and led to the partial regeneration of the harbour area. Such was the success of the Galway welcoming of the race in 2008 that the city was chosen as the finish line for the 2011/2012 Volvo Ocean Race (photo: Volvo Ocean Race).

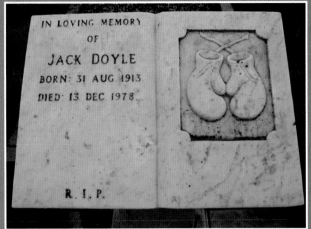

Once great athletes have retired and then passed away, what remains is the memory of their sporting prowess. Few athletes have their sporting lives celebrated on their headstones, but such commemoration when it does happen forms an intriguing part of our sporting heritage. The grave of legendary boxer, Jack Doyle, in Cobh, is decorated with a pair of boxing gloves, calling to mind the profession through which the 'Gorgeous Gael' first found fame (photo: Irish Sporting Heritage).

Above: In many cases, original playing fields from the early years of sport have been lost. Many such fields were often leased for a game or a season and were, in essence, always temporary. That said, these historical sites have great importance and some have been commemorated. Here, the site of the first All-Ireland football final in 1888 is marked with a plaque. The field on which the game would have been played now lies beneath the concrete and steel of the Donnybrook bus garage (photo: Damien Murphy).

Left: Handball alleys were built across the country in the nineteenth and early twentieth centuries. It was a hugely popular game, but with the move to indoor alleys, many of the outdoor alleys have been abandoned to the elements, converted for other uses or else demolished. Here at Maide Ban, Cavan, a former alley is used as a storage facility (photo: Áine Ryan, Irish Handball Alley Project).

When stadia are updated and remodelled, there is little in the way of recycling. Sometimes items such as floodlights are transplanted to new homes, but here an entire stand was moved. During the rebuilding of Croke Park in the 1990s, the decision was made to preserve the historic Nally Stand and move it north from Dublin to its new home at Pairc Colmcille, home of the Carrickmore GAA club in Tyrone (photo: Martin Gallagher, An Charraig Mhór GFC).

unimpeded. Again, as with Kilmainham, the object of the exercise, in heritage terms, is to preserve it as it was, and is, for future generations.

The same cannot be said for most sporting sites. As the majority are the ongoing homes of sports, players and spectators, they have to evolve constantly to support contemporary requirements. Stands that house thousands of spectators have to be safe. Facilities for players have to be state of the art. Clubhouses have to grow to accommodate bars, restaurants, hotel rooms, banqueting suites and even conference venues. What this means is that sporting spaces, as they are constantly evolving, cannot be preserved in aspic in the way of many other types of heritage buildings and spaces. Given that, we have to rethink what heritage means within the sporting context, and reach a definition that can be applied to sporting heritage.

What we suggest then is a twofold approach. First, we acknowledge sites that contain a built heritage, which have significant architectural importance. These sites are fewer in Ireland than elsewhere, but those that do exist are worthy of attention and preservation. Second, and more generally, there is a heritage attached to sporting sites, but not obvious in terms of the architectural significance. In

The modernist and art deco architectural styles largely, with a few notable exceptions, passed Ireland by. In Tramore, the Hydro was built in 1948 to include swimming baths and a restaurant. On opening, the Hydro employed seven people: a manageress was paid at the rate of £5 a week, a typist and bookkeeper was paid £2 a week, a physiotherapist was paid £8 8s a week, two bath attendants, one male and one female, were paid £5 10s a week each, a power plant attendant was paid £3 10s a week and a female general worker was paid £2 a week. Sadly the Hydro was demolished, and an exceptional part of the town's modernist architecture disappeared (photo: Waterford County Museum).

this, we argue that sporting sites, many of which have existed in situ for over a century, are important for the games that were played there, the historical forces that shaped them and the people who played and watched. In this vein, we suggest that sporting sites are heritage sites. This is not necessarily contingent on whatever stands on the site now (in all likelihood, modern, functional structures), but rather in terms of what has happened there. A string of questions can be asked of each site, such as what classes passed through, what role did politics play, how did the economy and business shape the site, what significant sporting events took place there, and how were gender relationships configured there?

What is striking from any examination of Irish sporting sites is both the rate of change and the high number of abandoned sporting places. Sporting sites are in a constant state of transformation, given the demands that are made of them. For some, that rate of change, particularly in the wider society, or else in terms of technology, means that they become obsolete. Prize-fighting venues, bull rings, dog and cock fighting pits, as well as a high number of outdoor handball alleys, outdoor swimming pools and racecourses

Opened in 1926, Glenmalure Park was the home of Shamrock Rovers until 1987, when it was sold. The site was purchased by a developer and is now occupied by housing. Despite the loss of the ground, many Rovers fans felt that Glenmalure Park in Milltown was the club's true home. This photograph of the ground was taken shortly after it had been vacated by the club. The sense of loss amongst supporters was such that they collected money and erected a monument to permanently mark the site of their old home. (photos: (above) Fergus Desmond, Shamrock Rovers Heritage Trustee; (right): Irish Sporting Heritage).

have all closed and have either been replaced by new buildings with a different function, or else fallen into a state of dereliction. These departures from the sporting landscape have been the product of changing social morals, in the case of fighting venues, the move indoors for swimmers and handball players, and the lack of economic profit for some racecourses and the sport of speedway. Just because a sporting site is here today does not mean that it will be there tomorrow (as any Shamrock Rovers fan will tell you). Even for the major sports of the GAA, rugby and soccer, a new stadium delivered now is built with the expectation that it will have a lifetime of no more than three or four decades. So while now we look with wonder at the recently completed Aviva stadium, it probably will be demolished and rebuilt again in the lifetime of today's forty-year-olds.

Many sporting sites have a heritage value, not of themselves, but rather for what took place there. Croke Park, in addition to all the sport that has been witnessed there, was the location of the 1920 Bloody Sunday killings. Lansdowne Road was the home of international rugby and soccer, and all the heroic feats that took place there, long before the Aviva Stadium was dreamt of. Crossmaglen Rangers ground was the site of British Army occupation through the years of the Troubles. College Park at Trinity has a long history of collegiate sport but is significant in the annals of cricket history as it is where W. G. Grace played in most of his Irish matches. The Rossenarra Stud Farm in Kilkenny, which has bred many notable racehorses, is where the most famous Grand National horse ever – Red Rum – was born. Ireland then, is packed with sites that have a sporting significance for a variety of reasons. As a result, no matter how we view these sites today, they speak to our wider historical and sporting past. They are the places where, put simply, things happened, and as such they cannot be moved elsewhere. They are the

sporting homes to our history, they are the locations of our collective memory.

In their entirety, sporting spaces talk of a nation at play. They reveal stories of how the railways moved us, of how the British army shaped the games we play and where we play them, and of the sporting feats that were undertaken. They tell us about our political, religious and gender identities, of how important schools and universities have been to our physical culture. They are the results of our forefathers adapting their games to fit the landscape, sometimes taming it, on other occasions working with it. They speak to the need to control crowds and charge entrance fees, the desire to build a bar or hotel to make money from the sports-goers. In essence, they tell the story of how all classes of Irish people chose to spend their leisure time, and the ways in which they facilitated their need to watch and play sport.

So should we preserve them? Are they iconic symbols of Ireland's heritage? On the issue of preservation, we argue that not everything that exists today has a historical or architectural value, and therefore the state should not intervene to list and preserve a myriad of sporting sites. That said, where does one draw the line? If handball alleys are taken as an example, the levels of dereliction and destruction that most outdoor alleys are suffering are clear to see. It would be unfeasible and unnecessary to preserve them all. But when do we see that we are down to the last handful of alleys, and intervene? It would be sad to see them all lost, and clearly some should be preserved as monuments to the ways people played, but on that basis, which ones do we select? For most existing sporting sites that are in regular use, the heritage argument comes a poor second to the needs of the people who use them day to day. Whether a major racecourse, local golf course, or private tennis club, all the managers of these facilities have to respond to the demands of their patrons, as well as to the letter of the law, in terms of health and safety concerns. As such, there will be few sporting sites existing today that will look the same in twenty or thirty years' time. The modernisation of facilities will have to take place, and the destruction of the historic and contemporary is inevitable. We argue throughout this book that sporting sites are iconic symbols of Ireland's heritage. They have been the venues for a nation at play, and as such deserve respect and an acknowledgement of their value and of what happened there, of the ways in which larger issues in society were replicated in the history of any given site. Such sites cannot, however, be preserved forever. Rather what we ask of the owners of sporting sites, be they associations, clubs, councils or even the state, is that in the pressing need to renew and refurbish, there is also an acknowledgement of the past.

While heritage is often understood in terms of the built environment, there are also sporting practices that can be considered as part of our heritage. Sports and games that were associated with the pub and the village green were common in Ireland until the early twentieth century. Some have survived and are still played, such as this local variant of skittles in Cavan (photo: Johnstown Central Library).

9

MAJOR SITES

AVIVA STADIUM, LANSDOWNE ROAD, DUBLIN

In its old incarnation prior to 2007, Lansdowne Road was the oldest sports stadium in Europe. It is also the world's oldest Rugby Union Test venue.

The land on which the Aviva Stadium now stands was taken on a 69-year lease from the Pembroke Estate by Henry William Dunlop at £60 per annum in 1872. Dunlop was full of energy and imagination and had founded the Irish Champion Athletics Club earlier in the year. A railway station was opened in Lansdowne Road in 1870 and this greatly enhanced the appeal of the site as a sports venue. Dunlop's intention was to lay out a cricket pitch, leaving enough ground for a proper cinder running path. However, it was athletics rather than cricket that dominated the early years of the stadium. Dunlop organised the first All-Ireland Athletics Championships in 1873. The Viceroy, Earl Spencer, officially opened the ground later that year and it rapidly became an important venue for Dublin sporting events. It had an enclosed running path, cricket ground, 400-seat grandstand, sloping seats for 600 more, archery and croquet hut, gate lodge, and dressing rooms under the railway arch.

Dunlop formed a rugby team and facilities were laid out for the playing of the game in 1873–74. By the late 1880s rugby was unrivalled as the main sport at Lansdowne Road. The first interprovincial match was

A concrete grandstand was built in Lansdowne Road in 1925–26 by the architects Donnelly, Moore, Keatinge and Robinson, who were also responsible for building the grandstand at Baldoyle Racecourse. It was as radically modern in its design in the 1920s as that of the Aviva Stadium almost ninety years later (photo: Ferro-Concrete, April 1930).

played there in 1876. Leinster beat Ulster by a goal and try to two tries. Two years later the ground hosted its first international rugby fixture, against England, but it would be 1887 before Ireland won a rugby match against England in Lansdowne Road. The kick-off was timed for 'after the arrival of the three o'clock train'. In the early twentieth century the Irish Rugby Football Association (IRFU) secured the lease of Lansdowne Road from the Pembroke Estate and the ground became still more associated with rugby football.

More concrete stands and terracing were added to Lansdowne Road and, although it could no longer be considered a state-of-the-art venue, it was in a better condition than most grounds in the country. As a result, from 1990, it became the home of international soccer matches as well as, traditionally, international ruby matches. It is photographed here in 1977 (photo: Dublin City Libraries).

When war was declared in August 1914, the Irish Rugby Union Volunteer Corps (IRUVC) was formed under the leadership of F. H. Browning, the President of the IRFU, and large numbers of men drilled nightly at Lansdowne Road. Over 600 went on to enlist and in particular to join a 'Pals' company of the 7th Royal Dublin Fusiliers. In October 1914 the Volunteer Corps played the Fusiliers, at Lansdowne Road, in a match attended by a huge and enthusiastic crowd. A memorial to the IRFU members who died in the First World War was erected on the inside of the external wall of the stadium. Planning permission for rebuilding of the stadium was conditional on the memorial being preserved. It is now located just outside the new Aviva Stadium media centre.

By the time soccer arrived in Dublin, a decade after Dunlop set up his multi-sport club, there was little room for it at Lansdowne Road. Also club rules barred anyone who was 'a mechanic, labourer or artisan' and this excluded many who played soccer. The headquarters of the Irish Football Association (IFA) were in Belfast and it was not until 1900 that an international soccer match was held in Dublin. Ireland lost to England 0–2. This was the only 32-county Ireland soccer international to be played at Lansdowne Road.

Dalymount Park had been built by the time the Belfast-based IFA next agreed to another international in Dublin, and then, in 1921 the Football Association of Ireland was established and the island fielded two international sides. Besides one Army Cup Final in the 1920s and the first home game by the Free State in 1927, soccer was not played at Lansdowne again until the 1960s. The Football Association of Ireland first leased the ground for international soccer matches in 1971, and from 1990 it has been used for the vast majority of home fixtures by the Republic of Ireland. It was at a soccer match in 1995 that England football hooligans threw seats and metal at

The ground leased on Lansdowne Road in 1872 was bounded by the railway line and the Dodder and Swan Rivers, as can clearly be seen in this aerial photograph taken in 2005. The development of the surrounding area also made it impossible for the Lansdowne Road stadium to expand. Nevertheless, in 2007 it was decided that the new stadium would continue on the same site (photo: Aviva Stadium).

The Aviva Stadium was opened in 2010. Its asymmetrical design is a result of the north end of the ground being in a densely populated residential area (photo: Aviva Stadium).

Irish fans in a response to a goal being scored by Ireland's David Kelly. The match was abandoned as a result.

Demolition of Lansdowne Road began in May 2007. In a €410 million venture by the IRFU and the FAI the reconstructed stadium opened in March 2010 under its new name, Aviva. It is one of the most expensive structures erected in the Republic of Ireland. The new 50,000-seater stadium was designed by Populous, the architects who had previously been involved in projects such as the Sydney Olympic Stadium and Arsenal's Emirates Stadium in London. The first fixture in the new stadium saw a Connacht/Munster rugby selection take on a Leinster/Ulster selection on 31 July 2010.

CROKE PARK, DUBLIN

Croke Park, seen here from the air in the 1940s, is a stadium that has had to adapt to its surroundings. With the canal at one end and the railway at the other, Croke Park could not develop as it wished, but rather had to build its stands and terraces without affecting the transport routes. The size and scale of the old open terraces of Hill 16, in the top right corner, are clearly shown here (photo: GAA Museum and Archive).

Without doubt the largest sporting venue in Ireland, Croke Park can also lay claim to being the most historically significant. When the GAA began life in 1884, it relied on various rented pitches to play its games, and even the early All-Ireland finals were moved from place to place. In 1896, the finals were played for the first time at the then City and Suburban Racecourse on Jones Road.

The City and Suburban Racecourse was a private facility owned by Maurice Butterly, and various attempts had been made by its owners to make it a going concern by hosting cycling races, athletics contests and horse races. It was the original home of Bohemians soccer club, and in 1901 the IFA Cup final was staged there. Despite all this activity Butterly could not garner enough business to make a profit. The arrival of the All-Ireland finals in 1896 helped the stadium's finances and also began the link between the Association and the site, which has endured for over a century.

In 1908 Butterly decided to sell the ground, and well-known GAA journalist and supporter of the Association

Above: The current Croke Park is one of the biggest stadia in Europe, in terms of capacity, and a testimony to the vision of the GAA who understood that the old ground had, by the 1990s, reached the end of its useful life. Designed to include conference suites, corporate boxes, restaurants and bars, as well as the GAA's own offices, Croke Park is very much a 21st-century stadium (photo: Croke Park Stadium).

Facing page: This picture from the 1970s shows how Croke Park had been developed. Rather than a wholesale rebuilding, as would happen from the 1990s, the GAA worked with what they had. The Hogan Stand remains unchanged, but the Cusack has, by this time, been redeveloped so that it sits under a single stand. Seating areas were expanded and the terraces on Hill 16 made more uniform (photo: GAA Museum and Archive).

Frank Dineen purchased it for £3,500. Dineen quickly developed the site, re-laying the pitches and building further terraces. By 1913, the ground had been renamed Croke Park, in honour of the GAA's founding patron. That year also saw Kerry and Louth face each other in the inaugural Croke Memorial tournament. In the event, forty special trains carried supporters to Dublin, and a crowd estimated at 35,000 filled the ground. Gate receipts of over £2,000 meant that the Central Council was in a position to buy the stadium from Dineen. The GAA now owned the jewel in its crown.

The close links between the stadium and the history of the nation began in concrete form in 1917 when a new terrace was built at the northern end of the ground. The material used was the rubble from buildings destroyed during the 1916 Rising, and the name given to the terrace was Hill 16. In 1920, political events impinged on the life of the stadium in a horrifying way. After British spies had been killed in Dublin on the morning of 21 November 1920, British forces sought reprisals and decided to attack a crowd gathered at Croke Park to watch Dublin play Tipperary. In the firing that ensued, thirteen spectators and the Tipperary captain, Michael Hogan, were killed. The day was named Bloody Sunday and the events memorialised in 1924, when the new stand built on the Jones Road side of the ground was named in honour of Michael Hogan. There is also a memorial on the concourse beneath the stand to all those who died.

The Hogan stand, opened in 1924, was built to house spectators attending the inaugural Aonach Tailteann, which took place that year. The stadium hosted the opening ceremony, and all the athletics and Gaelic games. The event was staged again in 1928 and 1932. That Croke Park was, until 2005, closed to foreign games, has never stopped it from hosting a wealth of non-GAA events. In the 1930s the doors of the ground were opened to a travelling rodeo circus, and it has also hosted the 1929 Catholic Emancipation centenary, an American football game in aid of the Red Cross in 1953, the 1961 Patrician Year celebrations, a five-day festival in 1966 to commemorate the fiftieth anniversary of the Rising, the Muhammad Ali versus Al Blue Lewis fight of 1972 and the Special Olympics in 2003. The stadium also plays host to many of the leading music acts each summer.

In the 1990s, following concerns about crowd safety and the age of much of the stadium's structure, the decision was made to rebuild Croke Park. Work took fourteen years, during which time all scheduled games went ahead as normal, and completed in 2005. The stadium's capacity, after the reconstruction, was 82,300, one of the biggest in the European Union. During the process of building the new stadium, the GAA also built a museum and archive and, in doing so, became one of the first sporting bodies in Ireland to have a purpose-built heritage visitor attraction.

With the closure of Lansdowne Road, ready for its transformation into the Aviva Stadium, the decision was taken to open Croke Park to the games of rugby and soccer in 2005. In the event, games were played there from 2007 until 2010, when work was completed on the Aviva. Croke Park is such an iconic site in Irish life that during the state visit of Queen Elizabeth II, she made a highly symbolic trip there.

More than simply a sports venue, Croke Park is the national home of the country's largest sporting and cultural organisation, it has been shaped by and sadly played host to the momentous events of Ireland's history, and stands as a testament to modern stadium design and the work of an Association that built it and made it a success.

The Curragh, Kildare

Special trains were organised by railway companies, allowing spectators to travel to race meetings at reduced costs. Horses were often transported for free. Excursion trains also stopped at the Curragh in order to transport people to other racing events at courses such as Down Royal (photo: Irish Sporting Heritage).

The entire area of the Curragh of Kildare was declared a national monument in 1995 in recognition of its significance in Irish sporting and historical life. Cuireach means the place of the running horse. Chariot races were held there in the third century and the first recorded flat race took place in 1727. The Curragh is the home of the Turf Club and is at the heart of the Irish bloodstock industry. It was the location of the first Irish Derby in 1866 and, beyond the racecourse, was the site of the first golf course to be laid out in Ireland, in 1852.

Horse racing was one of the first sports to become regulated and the founding of the Turf Club in Kildare in 1790 helped to secure the position of the Curragh as the premier flat racing venue in Ireland. This was also the first year of the publication of the Racing Calendar that listed race meetings, promoted a unified code of rules and advanced the authority of the Turf Club. The only year it has not been published is 1798. Political activity has always been intertwined with the history of the Curragh. In May 1798, 300 United Irishmen were shot there on a place called the Gibbet Rath and the following month the races were not held 'owing to the disturbed state of the country'. It was to evoke the memory of this event that Daniel O'Connell chose the Standhouse as the location for his Repeal meeting at the Curragh forty-five years later.

In the mid-nineteenth century the British administration decided to create a permanent camp to accommodate 10,000 men and the Curragh became the largest military station in Ireland. Nevertheless, in 1868 the Curragh of Kildare Act preserved the use of the land for the purpose of horse racing and the presence of the horse racing fraternity and of such a large military presence combined to make the Curragh a crucial location for the development of sport in Ireland.

The visit by King George IV to the Curragh in 1821 was an occasion of great excitement. The sum of £3,000 was raised to erect a new stand, and marquees were installed for the masses. The King presented The Royal Whip, with a handle covered in finely wrought solid gold shamrocks, to the Curragh, one of the finest trophies in racing. The railway station (on the far right) closed in 1977 (photo: National Library of Ireland).

On race days, courses such as the Curragh are thronged with crowds socialising, betting and watching the races (photo: Curragh Racecourse).

Some of the most famous races in the world take place at the Curragh, including the Irish Guinness Festival, the Irish Derby, the Irish Oaks and the Irish St Ledger (photo: Peter Higgins).

Plans have been in place to build a new grandstand at the Curragh to accommodate 50,000 people. The old stand will be demolished (photo: Peter Higgins).

The first excursion train ever to be run by the Great Southern and Western Railway (GSWR) was to the Curragh, for the race meeting of 15 October 1846. The introduction of third class tickets at 2s 6d the following year encouraged 1,000 people to travel from Dublin for the races. In 1850 GSWR funded a railway plate, and for many years the Railway Stakes was the principle railway-sponsored event in Ireland. In 1853 a standhouse at the racecourse was built by the railway architect Sanction Wood and funded by GSWR, at a cost of £3,000, in compensation for the appropriation of land for the Dublin-to-Cashel line. The racing fraternity proved itself formidable in battles with the interests of both the army and the rail companies.

Sports of all kinds have been played at the Curragh Camp. In 1841 the Duke of Wellington ordered that cricket grounds be laid out in barracks throughout the kingdom for the use of officers and other ranks, and by 1866 two cricket pitches had been laid out at the Curragh. Boxing competitions, polo, football matches and golf competitions were among the many games played in garrisons. In 1939 a GAA pitch was laid out in the Curragh camp, reportedly with many of the old British army cannon buried beneath the sodding. In the 1940s two motor racing circuits were constructed at the Curragh and attracted huge crowds to car and motorcycle events until racing ceased in 1954.

A garrison golf club was formed in 1883 and is the second oldest golf club in Ireland (the oldest being Royal Belfast, founded in 1881). A ladies' nine-hole course was laid out in 1897. There was neither entry fee nor subscription but membership was confined to officers of the British Curragh Garrison. The golf course had to be changed many times in the early years to meet military requirements. Barracks, parade grounds, firing ranges and the Water Tower now stand where there were once fairways and greens. The club continues to play over an area encompassing trenches dug by soldiers preparing for the First World War, a cavalry camp and the abattoir (demolished in 1996), which dated back to the year of the camp's foundation.

Following the treaty of 1921 the land of the Curragh passed from the British Crown to Irish ownership and is now owned by the Department of Defence. It continues as a vast and rich area of sporting heritage.

DALYMOUNT PARK, DUBLIN

Dalymount Park, shown here in 1977, was acquired by Bohemian Football Club in 1901. Its concrete stand, turnstiles and boundary wall were added in 1927 by architects Donnelly, Moore, Keatinge and Robinson (photo: Dublin City Libraries).

Dalymount Park is located on Dublin's north side. It is the home of Bohemian Football Club and was the venue for Republic of Ireland international games until they were moved to Lansdowne Road in 1990. Bohemian Football Club was founded in 1890 and acquired its first home ground two years later when a private pitch was secured at Jones Road on an area later occupied by Belvedere Rugby Football Club, beside Croke Park. The advantage of acquiring the ground was that admission prices could be charged by the club at significant matches. The formation of the Leinster Senior Cup in 1893 also assisted the growth in spectators for Dublin soccer.

In September 1901, just over a decade after the club was founded, Bohemian Football Club moved to a new ground, known locally as Pisser Dignam's Field, in Phibsborough, Dublin. This open land, with a vegetable plot on one side, was renamed Dalymount Park and officially opened by the Lord Mayor of Dublin. Bohemian's new ground consisted of a field surrounded by corrugated iron with ropes marking out the pitch. A tent acted as a changing room. Nevertheless 5,000 people turned up for the first match, against Shelbourne, and gate receipts were £40. Bohemians won 4–2. International clubs were invited to the ground and, within months of its

Right: In order to maximise the economic potential of sporting grounds it was important to secure the site and obscure the view of those who had not paid an entrance fee (photo: Damien Murphy).

Above: This is a programme from the Ireland v Germany in October 1936. It belongs to Eddie Power whose grandfather was at the game.

Right: Due to the poor condition of the grounds, international matches have not been held at Dalymount since 1990 (photo: Damien Murphy).

opening, Glasgow Celtic played at Dalymount Park. In 1921 the Football Association of Ireland (FAI) was founded, marking a break with the Belfast-based Irish Football Association (which had been founded in 1880). The new association formed its own league and Bohemian was the first club to signify its intention to join.

In line with developments at other sporting venues across the country the facilities in Dalymount Park were significantly improved in the 1920s and 1930s. Modern concrete design increased the economic potential of these grounds and replaced the corrugated iron surround. Dalymount's boundary walls, turnstiles and stands, built in 1927 for £2,520, were designed by Donnelly, Moore and Keatinge, the architects responsible for the grandstand at Lansdowne Road in the previous year. The serious aspirations for Dalymount were further illustrated by the fact that in 1931 the famous stadium architect, Archibald Leitch, designed the extension to the grandstand and terrace work. Leitch had also designed a new stand for Windsor Park in Belfast in 1930. These renovations required a huge financial commitment from the club,

much of it from loans personally guaranteed by individual members. Soccer was an amateur sport, and it was not until 1969 that Bohemians played their first competitive match with paid players in the side.

Dalymount Park has hosted international, European and FAI cup games. One of its more infamous matches was between the Irish Free State XI and Germany in 1936. Ireland won 5–2. Newspaper reports recorded that at the close of the match a huge crowd rushed across the ground and took up position in front of the grandstand where the German officials were located, 'and lustily cheered the visitors, hundreds of arms being raised to the Nazi salute'. Dalymount's record attendance was 48,000, for an Irish international game against England on 19 May 1957. A last-minute equaliser gave England a 1–1 draw.

In later decades the poor state of the facilities in Dalymount Park has meant that the ground no longer hosts international matches. The downturn in the Irish economy means that it is unlikely to undergo significant redevelopment in the immediate future and it continues to struggle financially.

Dalymount Park is located in a densely populated part of Dublin's north side. It is a focal point of the Phibsborough community and is overlooked by St Peter's Church (photo: Peter O'Doherty).

NORTH OF IRELAND CRICKET CLUB, ORMEAU, BELFAST

In 2001 the North of Ireland Cricket Club ('North') moved from its ground at Ormeau in Belfast. The relocation to Deramore Park, and the merger with Collegians to form Belfast Harlequins, was the end of 140 years of cricket in the area. The North of Ireland Club had seen some turbulent years – many of its records were lost during the extensive bombing of Belfast in 1941 – and its history reflects the wider experiences the city.

North of Ireland Cricket Club was officially founded in 1859 at a meeting at the Royal Hotel in Belfast. The membership entrance fee was set at two guineas with a further annual subscription of one guinea. Members were to be elected by ballot, 'one black bean to exclude'. The ground was originally leased in the 1860s from the Marquis of Donegall whose son-in-law, the Earl of

Shaftesbury, inherited the property and maintained a very good relationship with the club.

In the early 1860s the North's ground lay between the Ormeau Road and the River Lagan on the city side of Lavinia Street. The club was described in the 1865 *Handbook of Cricket in Ireland* as having the best ground in the country. In 1866 the club moved to the ground it would occupy until 2001. The opening was marked with a two-day match against Na Shuler XL (an Irish travelling club), which counted among its later members Charles Stewart Parnell. During its history the club would host forty-three internationals. The ground was also used for athletics meetings and set up for rugby football in the winter months. This provided additional income for the club.

Australian cricketers, seen here in 1938, first played at the Ormeau ground in 1883 and they were the last team to take on an Irish side there before the ground closed (photo: North of Ireland Cricket Club).

The extension to the pavilion was opened in 1959. Despite shortages in the years after the Second World War, the club used the 'Victory Fund' to improve the facilities within the club (photo: North of Ireland Cricket Club)

The political circumstances of the early twentieth century impacted on the club and at a meeting of the North of Ireland Football Club called in December 1913 it was agreed that: 'all matches for the second half of the season should be cancelled so that members who are identified with the Ulster Volunteer Force and the Unionist Clubs might have more leisure to devote themselves to the work of drilling and otherwise preparing for eventualities.' Cricket, however, continued at Ormeau and, of the thirty-one matches arranged for 1914, only nine were cancelled.

Like many sporting clubs across Ireland, North found that the First World War took a significant toll on its members. Of the 253 who took the colours 60 died and a memorial was unveiled to them in the grounds. At the end of the Second World War the Club Committee inaugurated a Victory Fund designed to wipe off the Club's debts and 'formulate plans to perpetuate the memory of those members who have fallen in the service of their country by making North a better North'. Lord Shaftesbury extended the lease on the ground by 10,000

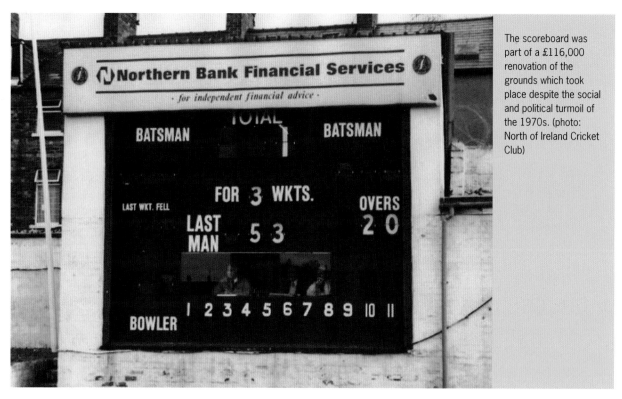

The scoreboard was part of a £116,000 renovation of the grounds which took place despite the social and political turmoil of the 1970s. (photo: North of Ireland Cricket Club)

years in order to perpetuate the memory of those members of the club who died in two world wars and in a very real sense the ground itself became a memorial to their sacrifice.

The location of the North of Ireland Cricket Club off the Ormeau Road in Belfast meant that it could not escape the impact of the conflict in Northern Ireland. In the first half of the 1970s the civil unrest led to destruction of the property and meant that social activities were almost impossible. In 1973 the Northern Cricket Union decided it could no longer stage the Senior Cup Final at Ormeau in view of the civil unrest and this event was transferred to the Downpatrick CC ground. The resilience of the club, and indeed of all sporting facilities in Belfast at this time, is suggested in the fact that extensive renovations were nevertheless carried out during the 1970s, including an additional squash court, ladies' changing rooms and a new cricket score box.

Sectarian attacks continued, however, and in 1997 the Centenary Pavilion was badly damaged by a fire, which also caused some damage to the main pavilion. By the beginning of the twentieth-first century the land off the Ormeau Road was of a premium to property developers. Changes to the rugby season further strengthened the argument for moving to a new ground that would accommodate the playing of both cricket and rugby simultaneously. The final cricket match was played against Australia in August 2001. Rain stopped play.

THE NATIONAL BOXING STADIUM, DUBLIN

The National Boxing Stadium was built by the voluntary efforts of the Irish Amateur Boxing Association. This photograph shows the opening of the stadium in 1939 by the Minister of Defence, Frank Aiken (photo: National Boxing Stadium).

Dan Donnelly has possibly the most unusual place in Ireland's sporting heritage. A spot in Kildare bears his name and his right arm has had an extensive life since the boxer's death. On 13 December 1815 thousands watched as Donnelly defeated the English bare-knuckle boxing champion George Cooper in the natural amphitheatre in the Curragh. Over 70,000 people attended Donnelly's funeral in 1820; his grave, in the Royal Hospital Kilmainham, was subsequently robbed and the surgeon who purchased his body recognised it as that of a pugilist. The right arm was preserved and has been on public view in different forums ever since. Donnelly's Hollow in Kildare, where the fight took place, is marked by a stone memorial and can still be visited today.

Prize fighting has formed an important part of Irish sporting life. Pugilism (fist-fighting) was one of the first

Donnelly's Hollow in the Curragh, County Kildare, is a natural amphitheatre. A monument marks the place where, on 13 December 1815, thousands watched as Dan Donnelly defeated the English bare-knuckle boxing champion George Cooper (photo: Peter Higgins).

In 2001 the stadium was extensively refurbished and the front of the building transformed. This photograph shows the entrance on South Circular Road as it is today (photo: Damien Murphy).

The Irish Amateur Boxing Association is the only amateur boxing association in the world to own, control and run its own national arena and stadium (photo: Damien Murphy).

Irish boxers have won twelve medals at the Olympic Games. They train at a high-performance facility next to the National Boxing Stadium, which can be seen in this photograph (photo: Damien Murphy).

sports to have a written code of rules and was heavily commercialised by the eighteenth century. However, it was increasingly under pressure from the authorities in the nineteenth century and large gatherings to watch contests were considered riotous assemblies. Bare-knuckle boxing had declined in popularity by the 1890s and the first gloved boxing heavyweight championship was held in America in 1892 between John Sullivan (a son of Irish immigrants) and 'Gentleman Jim' Corbett. The Irish played a prominent part in American boxing history and tales of their successes have continued to nurture the boxing tradition in Ireland.

The implementation of the Queensbury Rules (published in 1867) helped to establish the respectability of boxing and, by the twentieth century, it was seen as character building for working class youths. Boxing clubs were established in the premises of many Catholic Young Men's Societies throughout Ireland. These were similar to working men's clubs and often included billiards and snooker tables; they can still be found in several towns, including Youghal and Cavan.

In 1911 the Irish Amateur Boxing Association (IABA) was founded and was confined in its early days to a small number of clubs. The objective of the Association was the social, moral and physical education of its members; and the organisation, control and promotion of the Olympic Sport of Amateur Boxing. The formation of the Free State in 1922 gave an extra impetus to the development of boxing in Ireland as it was seen as central to the physical training of the new army and police force.

In 1936 the IABA decided to embark on the construction of its own National Boxing Arena. A Board of Trustees was appointed, which included Frank Aiken, Minister for Defence, and Major General W. R. E. Murphy, Police Commissioner. Twenty-five square feet of land in Griffith Barracks were leased from the government

for the purpose. The cost of the building was £12,000 and the architects, Jones and Kelly, the surveyor and solicitor gave their services for free. The stadium was designed so that its doors opened onto the South Circular Road and in such a way that extensions might be built onto it in the future. Based on the boxing stadium in Liverpool, the arena had a seating capacity of 2,400. The National Stadium was formally opened in March 1939 by the Minister for Defence and blessed by the parish priest, the Venerable Archdeacon Grimes.

Shortly after its opening the Arena hosted the last European Boxing Championship to be held before the Second World War. On 22 April 1939 Jimmy Ingle of Ireland beat Niiki Obermauer of Germany to win the European Flyweight title, and Paddy Dowdall beat Poland's Anton Czostak to win the European Featherweight title. Ireland also hosted the first post-war European Senior Championships in 1947 at the National Stadium. Gearóid Ó Colmáin became the European Heavyweight Champion.

Boxing is one of the most important sports in Ireland and has been responsible for over half its Olympic medals since 1922. However, many clubs are located in sports complexes or above business premises and have made little contribution to Ireland's built sporting heritage. This has made the building of the National Stadium even more significant. It served to unify and co-ordinate the boxing provincial councils, county boards and clubs, as it has acted as a focal point for the administration of amateur boxing in Ireland. There are now approximately 350 active clubs throughout the country; however, boxing continues to be concentrated primarily in urban areas, particularly Dublin, Belfast and Cork.

The Irish Amateur Boxing Association is the only amateur boxing association in the world to own, control and run its own national arena and stadium

SHELBOURNE PARK, DUBLIN

What began life as a soccer stadium has become identified as the home of greyhound racing in Ireland and the venue of the most important annual race, the Irish Greyhound Derby. The main stand offers all the modern facilities, including bars and restaurants, while the outdoor betting ring remains as a marker of the more traditional night out (photo: Irish Greyhound Board).

Located in Dublin 4, between Ringsend and Ballsbridge, Shelbourne Park is nowadays known as a greyhound racing track. While the dogs were the reason the stadium was built to its current configuration, and have been the constant residents since 1927, they have not always been the sole occupiers. Shelbourne soccer club was founded in 1895, and joined the League of Ireland in 1904. Originally the club played its games at St Mary's Field, but in 1913 began playing its games at Shelbourne Park. The club stayed at

the Park until 1948. During their occupancy, they won five league and two cup titles. Shelbourne Park was also used for the FAI Cup final replays of 1927 and 1929.

Speedway racing first appeared in Ireland in 1902, when races took place around an oval cinder track in Ashtown. The sport came into its own, particularly in Britain, where races took place at greyhound tracks under lights, in the 1920s and 1930s. After Harold's Cross opened as a greyhound track in 1928, a series of speedway

Above: Once greyhound racing had established itself in the late 1920s at Shelbourne, the facilities were tailor made for the next exciting modern sport to take place on the sanded oval: speedway. The Shelbourne Tigers raced from 1950 until 1954, but despite promising early crowds, there were insufficient spectators to keep the business going (photo: Irish Greyhound Board).

Right: A programme for the Shelbourne Tigers, from 1950 (photo: Irish Greyhound Board).

meetings were attempted, but do not seem to have gathered the necessary crowds to make it sustainable. The most serious attempt at introducing the sport took place in the 1950s, when the Wimbledon team was brought to Ireland to compete at Shelbourne Park. The man behind the idea was promoter Ronnie Green, who owned the Wimbledon Dons team; in Shelbourne they raced against other British teams under the name the Shelbourne Tigers. Initially crowds were good, and an Irish team, the Dublin

Eagles, was set up in Chapelizod, but enthusiasm was short lived and crowds soon fell off. By 1954, speedway no longer took place. Attempts were made in 1961 and 1970 to revive the sport at Shelbourne, but again these failed.

Shelbourne Park then, although a home to soccer and speedway, is really known for one thing: greyhound racing. Greyhound racing first came to Britain at Belle Vue in Manchester in July 1926. It was seen as the ideal sport of its age. It mixed technology (the electric hare and the lit

Shelbourne is located across from the Aviva Stadium, and racegoers attending a night at the dogs have the best view of it anywhere in the city (photo: Damien Murphy).

track for night-time races) with an adaptation of traditional sport (coursing), and allowed people, given that the stadia involved were usually purpose built, to socialise, eat, drink and gamble while they enjoyed the races. Such was the success of Belle Vue, which was regularly attended by Irish punters and dog enthusiasts, that two Belfast bookmakers, Joe Shaw and Hugh McAlinden, decided to open the first Irish track at Celtic Park in Belfast, with the inaugural meeting taking place in 18 April 1927.

The first meeting at Shelbourne took place a month later, on 14 May 1927, and was organised by Paddy O'Donoghue, Jerry Collins, Patsy McAlinden and Jim Clarke. The opening meeting was attended by a crowd of 10,000, which led *The Irish Times* reporter in attendance to complain that 'there was much congestion in front of the stands on Saturday, and it would have been more comfortable if the crowd had been better distributed'. His solution, and taking his cue from the arrangement of crowds at horse racing meetings, was a series of reserved enclosures dictated by price. The suggestion was never acted on.

Shelbourne always has been the premier track in Irish greyhound racing. The Irish Derby was first run there in 1930 (won by Guideless Joe), and has, with a few alternative venues, been run at Shelbourne ever since. In 1932, the Oaks was introduced as the second Irish

Betting remains a prime reason for going to the dogs for many patrons of Shelbourne. While they line up to watch the bookies make the odds, above them diners sit in the warmth of the restaurant enjoying a different kind of evening (photo: Damien Murphy).

greyhound classic, and in 1960, the Grand National (won in 1981 by Face the Mutt, the first dog to go on and win the British equivalent). All the major dogs from across the decades have run at Shelbourne Park, including the legendary Mick the Miller, who suffered the ignominy of coming second in a race to Odd Blade in the Easter Cup.

Over the decades Shelbourne Park has been constantly updated. While facilities were fairly basic through to the 1960s, 1969 saw the opening of the first major redevelopment of the track. A stand was erected to hold 15,000, the Long Bar introduced on the first floor and televisions fitted around the stand so that patrons could watch the races without venturing outside. A restaurant was also introduced on the ground floor of the stand. Such facilities would now be considered standard as, since the

1990s, Bord na gCon, the Irish Greyhound Board (which was established by the government to run the sport and administer its facilities in 1958), has focused on selling a night at the dogs as a social outing with first class facilities on offer. Shelbourne Park reflects that with its most recent stand featuring a wide range of dining and drinking options: the fun seekers upstairs behind the glass, the serious greyhound followers downstairs with access to the track. The policy has been incredibly successful, and while many British tracks have closed down in recent years, the Irish tracks have all now been updated and modernised. The Irish Greyhound Derby, held annually at Shelbourne, is one of the richest greyhound races in the world, and is one event each year guaranteed to fill the stadium.

ROYAL DUBLIN SOCIETY (RDS) SHOWGROUNDS, DUBLIN

The Royal Dublin Society was founded in 1731 by members of Ireland's ruling ascendancy, with the aim of improving knowledge and practices in agriculture and industry. In 1815 the Society purchased Leinster House in Dublin and remained there until 1923 when the fledgling Irish government purchased the site for £68,000. It was on the grounds of Leinster Lawn that the first Dublin Horse Show took place in 1864.

The Society's current site in Ballsbridge (purchased in 1877) has been the venue for rugby, soccer, cycling, wrestling and tennis as well as agricultural shows, exhibitions, concerts, and, in 1981, the Eurovision Song Contest. However, the Horse Show remains the premier event in its calendar. It is the largest equestrian event in Ireland. The Horse Show was a commercial success from the outset largely due to the 'leaping' competitions designed to test the suitability of horses for the hunting field. The Horse Show became a significant social event and was regularly attended by the Lord Lieutenant. The upper echelons of fashion gathered in the RDS and were described in 1903 as 'bewildering in their variety, beauty and brilliancy'.

A continuous horse jumping course was constructed in 1881 when the Horse Show moved to Ballsbridge. It included a high hurdle, a water jump and a stone-wall jump. A stand was also erected to hold 800 people. The opening of a railway siding in 1893 meant that the Horse Show was accessible to travellers from across the country and that livestock could be easily transported to the site. Special railway excursions were organised for those attending the show and the crowds included all sections of country life mingling with their urban counterparts.

The statue of Hibernia or Minerva was designed by the leading Dublin sculptor Edward Smyth in 1798. It was originally over the entrance of the Dublin Society's premises on Hawkins Street and was then moved to Leinster House, finally resting in Ballsbridge (photo: Damien Murphy).

By the outbreak of the First World War, show jumping was well established as a national sport rather than simply a test for prospective purchasers of horses for the hunt. However, the premises at Ballsbridge were requisitioned at the outbreak of war and the army remained in occupation until 1919. The grounds of the RDS were also occupied

Until 1951 teams in the Horse Show consisted of military officers (photo: Royal Dublin Society).

The Dublin Horse Show moved to Ballsbridge in 1880 and soon became a central part of the social calendar (photo: National Library of Ireland).

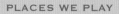

The covered Anglesea Stand is the oldest stand in the RDS (photo: Damien Murphy).

by the military during the Second World War. Nevertheless war charities used jumping competitions as a way of raising funds so the sport continued to thrive during wartime. At the resumption of show jumping in the RDS in 1919 women were finally allowed to enter competitions.

Membership of the Royal Dublin Society flourished in the early years of the Irish state and the introduction of the first international show jumping competition in1926 greatly enhanced attendance at the Horse Show. Ninety-three thousand people gathered to see the inaugural Nations' Cup for the Aga Khan Challenge trophy. Until 1951 the teams consisted of military officers so in its early years the Nations' Cup also offered an opportunity to demonstrate the skills of the new Irish Army, particularly through the Irish Army Equestrian School.

The Simmonscourt extension to the RDS in 1956 accommodated an increasing number of horses and a pavilion was constructed at a cost of £1.5 million. The stone walls within the jumping course were removed in the 1960s to make way for open-air concerts and the arena's capacity has expanded to 18,250. The RDS is also the home of Leinster Rugby and was home to Shamrock Rovers between 1990 and 1996. Hundreds of students in Ireland associate the smell of horses with sitting examinations, as both University College Dublin and Trinity College Dublin use the RDS as the location for their exams.

Temporary stands are now a common feature in the RDS as it hosts a variety of sporting and musical events (photo: Damien Murphy).

WINDSOR PARK, BELFAST

Windsor Park is the home of Linfield Football Club. It opened in 1905 and gets its name from the area of Belfast in which it stands. The stadium is also the venue for the home matches of the Northern Ireland football team. In common with many football teams in the early years of soccer, Linfield grew out of the workplace. In 1886 a group of workers at the Ulster Spinning Company in the Sandy Row, Belfast, asked for permission to form a team and to use the ground at the back of the mill called 'the meadow'. Soccer was slow to develop in Ireland but the industrial environment of Ulster meant that teams grew more rapidly in the northeast than elsewhere in the country. Industrial workers had incomes and free time, which helped to garner support for codified games such as soccer. The first Association Football match in Ireland took place in Belfast in 1878 and Cliftonville, Ireland's oldest soccer club, was founded the following year. It leased its current ground, Solitude, in 1890–91.

Linfield Football Club ('The Blues') had an itinerant beginning and it was not until 1904 that it purchased its own ground off the Lisburn Road where it still resides. A seated stand on the south terrace was installed in 1907 and an unreserved grandstand in 1909. A concrete boundary fence was erected in the early 1920s.

In 1929 an ambitious new grandstand and dressing rooms were developed by the well-known stadium architect Archibald Leitch, and the extension was officially opened with a match between Linfield and Glasgow Rangers (which ended in a scoreless draw). In 1937–38 the Irish Football Association (IFA) entered into a five-year contract for the staging of international matches at Windsor Park, an arrangement that was subsequently extended. A 100-year agreement was signed by the IFA in 1985 for Northern Ireland to play all home internationals at Windsor Park.

On Easter Tuesday, 15 April 1941, spectators watching Linfield play Distillery at Windsor Park noticed a lone Luftwaffe Junkers Ju-88 aircraft circling overhead. That night an estimated 180 aircraft participated in an assault lasting five and a half hours. Bombs fell on Belfast at an average rate of two every minute. The final death toll was at least 900, with 600 seriously injured. Gerry Morgan, the famous Cliftonville and Linfield player who had become a key member of the Linfield backroom staff, went to Windsor Park as the sirens sounded, such was his devotion to the ground.

The stadium's capacity was increased to 60,000 for international matches in the 1930s and this continued until the early 1960s. Floodlights were added in 1956 and new seating accommodation was included in the Railway Stand in 1966. A fire in the unreserved stand in 1982 saw the end of an integral part of Windsor Park's history. Fans had fond memories of crowding into the stand which was for many years emblazoned with advertisements for Gallaghers 'Blues' cigarettes. The slogan 'Ask for Blues everywhere' was naturally popular with supporters.

During Northern Ireland's qualification for the World Cup in 1982 the Secretary of State, Jim Prior, agreed to provide funding for 50 per cent of the capital cost of building a new stand, and a £2 million ultra-modern North Stand was opened in 1984. It is the only part of any soccer stadium that is owned by the IFA. A decision to provide a further £50,000 government funding to refurbish the South Stand in 1986 was heavily criticised by nationalist groups who argued that the main beneficiary would not be the Northern Ireland football team but

Windsor Park opened in 1905 and gets its name from the area of Belfast in which it stands (photo: Peter Higgins)

Linfield Football Club, which had not fielded a Catholic player since the early 1940s.

Sporting clubs are the product of their environment but sectarianism, present across the society, was a more pressing issue at Winsdor Park because it hosted Northern Ireland games. Linfield Football Club and the IFA have made significant and largely successful strides in recent years to address sectarianism and make Windsor Park, which now has a capacity of 27,000, an inclusive ground. In 2011 the Stormont administration allocated £25 million for the refurbishment of the stadium.

Above: The Railway Stand was opened in 1966 (photo: Peter Higgins).

Main photo: In 1937–38 the Irish Football Association entered into a five-year contract for the staging of international matches at Windsor Park, an arrangement that was subsequently extended and continues today (photo: Peter Higgins).

This mural outside the grounds at Windsor Park commemorates Northern Ireland players including George Best (photo: Peter Higgins).

10

SPORT-SPECIFIC SITES

FITZGERALD STADIUM, KILLARNEY

Fitzgerald Stadium, like many GAA grounds across Ireland, lacks aesthetic grandeur in conventional terms. But it represents layers of stories that are as rich in heritage as more ornate architectural sites. Almost every parish in Ireland has a dedicated GAA pitch. Grant and loan schemes within the organisation have helped to make this happen, but it is also primarily the result of the efforts of local volunteers. These pitches and clubhouses are the visual signature of sporting heritage in Ireland.

Fitzgerald Stadium was opened in 1936 and was part of a national 'boom' in the development of GAA grounds in that decade. Cusack Park in Ennis and Dr Cullen Park in Carlow opened in the same year and marked the GAA's move away from all-purpose sports grounds. Almost 30,000 people gathered for the official blessing of Fitzgerald Stadium by the Archbishop of Cashel, patron of the GAA. The opening ceremonies of Gaelic grounds generally underlined the political as well as the sporting importance of Gaelic games and linked the sites in the popular mind with national as well as local pride.

This combination of national, local and sporting pride came together in the naming of the ground. Dick Fitzgerald had an impressive GAA record and made a significant contribution to Kerry football. Born in Killarney in 1884, he won five All-Ireland medals and captained Kerry in 1913 and 1914. Fitzgerald was a player of immense technical skill in all aspects of the game and in 1914 he wrote the coaching manual *How to Play Gaelic Football*. Fitzgerald was an Irish Volunteer in 1916 and helped to organise Gaelic games while interned in Frongoch prisoner-of-war camp in Wales. In the years after his release he became the Kerry representative on the Munster and Central Councils of the GAA, a selector and referee. Fitzgerald's personal life became troubled in the years following the Civil War and after his playing career had ended, and he became a heavy drinker. On the Friday before the 1930 All-Ireland Final, under the influence of alcohol, he climbed onto the roof of Killarney courthouse and died from the subsequent fall. There was an outpouring of sympathy as the news of Fitzgerald's death became known and the decision of his club, Dr Crokes, to build a memorial park was given provincial and national support. The estimated cost of the development of Fitzgerald Stadium was £24,000 and approximately £3,000 was spent on labour.

Fitzgerald Stadium was blessed by the Archbishop of Cashel, patron of the GAA. The ceremonies surrounding the opening of Gaelic grounds reflected the virtually inseparable links between the GAA and the Catholic Church and marked them out as spaces which were semi-religious as well as social and political (photo: GAA Oral History Project).

Facilities were often very rudimentary, as can be seen from this photograph of the former changing rooms at Fitzgerald Stadium (photo: GAA Oral History Project).

The stadium was built, in large part, by patients of St Finian's Mental Hospital, which is situated beside the grounds. The use of patients was a controversial but not unique situation. Patients of St Dympna's Hospital in Carlow helped to build and maintain the cricket and hockey pitches, cycle and running tracks – which were for public use – in the hospital grounds. Dr Eamonn O'Sullivan, RSM of St Finian's, strongly believed that this was a progressive form of occupational therapy and fifty patients worked over several years to bring the stadium to completion. At this time there were over 1,000 patients in St Finians and O'Sullivan campaigned to get a handball court, a tennis court and billiard room for patients' use.

Fitzgerald Stadium has been under continual improvement. In the 1940s the terrace was extended and sideline seating provided for the first time. In the 1950s the embankment was erected on the town side of the ground, and in the 1960s dressing rooms were built. In 1977 a new stand and pavilion were erected at a cost of £100,000. It was decided to name the stand after Eamonn O'Sullivan. O'Sullivan had coached eight All-Ireland winning Kerry sides over five decades (from the 1920s to the 1960s) and was President of the Kerry Board of the Association. He had been Chairman of the Stadium Committee for many years and, late in his life, President.

It was not until 2001 that official recognition was given to the other men who built Fitzgerald Stadium. A plaque has been erected in honour of the contribution made by the patients of St Finians, 1930–1936

Fitzgerald Stadium as it is today. At its opening, it was described by the Archbishop of Cashel as, 'the finest playground in Ireland and can compare favourably with any stadium in the whole world' (photo: Irish Sporting Heritage).

CASEMENT PARK, BELFAST

Thousands gathered for the opening of Casement Park in 1953. This photograph shows a relay runner arriving with an urn of soil from Semple Stadium in Thurles and from Croke Park in Dublin (photo appeared in the *Andersonstown News* souvenir supplement celebrating fifty years of Casement Park).

Belfast's main GAA ground was opened with great ceremony in 1953. More than any other sporting venue in Ireland, Casement Park has been the site of political as well as sporting contests.

Prior to the purchase of Casement Park, the city's main GAA ground was Corrigan Park on the Whiterock Road. By the 1940s it was in need of significant renovation and, because of its location, had very limited access. It was therefore decided to purchase land at the edge of the city. Where Casement Park now stands on the Andersonstown Road was the last stop on the bus route. The area around the pitch was a dumping ground for the city's refuse and there was a fear that heavy concrete structures would sink. It was therefore decided to have no sideline seating and

Casement Park is the home of Antrim GAA. The Northern Ireland Assembly has recently announced a €71.4 million redevelopment of the grounds (photo: Peter Higgins).

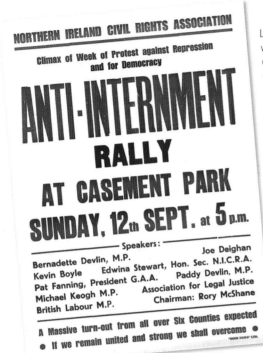

NORTHERN IRELAND CIVIL RIGHTS ASSOCIATION

Climax of Week of Protest against Repression and for Democracy

ANTI-INTERNMENT
RALLY
AT CASEMENT PARK
SUNDAY, 12th SEPT. at 5 p.m.

—— Speakers : ——

Bernadette Devlin, M.P.　　　　Joe Deighan
Kevin Boyle　　Edwina Stewart, Hon. Sec. N.I.C.R.A.
Pat Fanning, President G.A.A.　　Paddy Devlin, M.P.
Michael Keogh M.P.　　Association for Legal Justice
British Labour M.P.　　Chairman: Rory McShane

A Massive turn-out from all over Six Counties expected
● If we remain united and strong we shall overcome ●

Left: The introduction of internment without trial in August 1971 led to a campaign of civil disobedience organised by the Northern Ireland Civil Rights Association. Ten thousand people attended the rally in Casement Park in September 1971 (poster: Free Derry Museum).

Below: The turnstiles of Casement Park are a signature part of the Andersonstown Road. Although initially built on the edge of the city, the stadium now sits amid the shops and housing developments of one of the most populated parts of Belfast (photo: Peter Higgins).

This mural was commissioned to celebrate the 125th anniversary of the GAA. It was painted by Belfast artist Danny Diveney (photo: Peter Higgins).

COISTE CHONTAE AONTROMA CLG
125 BLIAIN
CLUICHÍ CULTÚR AGUS TEANGA

SEATING
(UNCOVERED)
←

STAND
(COVERED)
→

CASEMENT SOCIAL
CLUB NOW OPEN
→

instead a sloping terrace and one seated stand (built from scrap metal from the American airbase hangars at Lough Erne) were designed by former county player Danny McRandall. Money-raising efforts had begun during the Second World War and, by the time of the opening of the ground, £100,000 had been raised. Each club in Belfast was given an area of the grassy mounds surrounding the pitch to rake out and level, so each club contributed to the preparation of Casement Park.

The opening ceremony reflected the kind of lavish celebrations that accompanied the opening of many county grounds across Ireland. Cardinal D'Alton, Archbishop of Armagh and Primate of All Ireland, was driven up the Falls Road with a motorcade escort and was greeted by huge crowds lining the streets. The surrounding area had been decorated by papal flags, tricolours and bunting. A 20,000-strong crowd gathered in the grounds to watch the arrival of relay runners carrying an urn with soil from Semple Stadium in Thurles and Croke Park in Dublin. The Cardinal placed the soil in the centre of the pitch and, in the pouring rain, the Bishop of Down and Connor blessed the ground. Christy Ring played in the opening hurling match between Cork and Galway. Through its opening ceremony, and in being named after Roger Casement (educated in Ballymena) who was hanged for his part in the Easter Rising in 1916, the ground on the Andersonstown Road asserted its Irish nationalist credentials.

In its early years Casement Park provided a school for local children who were enrolled at the yet-to-be-built Holy Child School. Andersonstown expanded rapidly with the public housing boom of the post-war period and, in many ways, Casement Park was being built as Andersonstown was being built. Children were educated under the main stand, and played on the grassy banks and on the pitch during their break time.

Throughout the conflict in Northern Ireland Casement Park has been an important space of political dissent and of local unity. It held anti-internment rallies in the early 1970s and was occupied by the British Army for eighteen months during 1972 to 1973. For most of its history, however, it has been seen as a safe place for the expression of nationalist culture in County Antrim. It has been the venue for protests, rallies, festivals and commemorations, as well as sporting events.

West Belfast has expanded so that Casement Park now sits in its centre. It was built by local people and has been the site of the best and the worst aspects of their history. The 2011 announcement of a major government investment for Casement Park signals a new chapter in its story.

CORK COUNTY CRICKET CLUB, THE MARDYKE, CORK

The Mardyke is a tree-lined walkway beside the River Lee. It was first developed in 1719 and is called after a promenade in Amsterdam, 'Meer Dyke', meaning sea-dyke or embankment. This picture shows the Mardyke in the late nineteenth century (photo: Shay Curtin, with thanks to Richard T. Cooke).

The Mardyke area of Cork was first developed in 1719 and is called after a promenade in Amsterdam, 'Meer Dyke', meaning sea-dyke or embankment. The building of a tea house in 1722, the first of its kind in Cork, and the addition of fruit gardens and a gravel pathway turned the Mardyke into a fashionable walkway. Today it combines the natural beauty of the River Lee with a vast range of sports, including soccer, rugby, GAA, tennis and athletics.

The cricket pavilion on the Mardyke was built in 1879 and is unusual in Ireland's sporting heritage because most buildings of its vintage have either burnt down or been knocked down in the succeeding years. Cricket had arrived in this part of Cork thirty years earlier and has remained in the same location ever since. In its origins cricket was a sport of the privileged classes. It was diffused across the country under the patronage of the landed gentry and the

British army but then established itself among both urban and rural dwellers as a popular alternative to tennis and golf clubs, which often had more restricted membership rules. By the second half of the nineteenth century cricket had become probably the most popular game to be played in Ireland. Its subsequent demise is often ascribed to the impact of the political upheavals of Land League agitation in the 1880s and the rise of the GAA. However, the pattern of decline was not uniform across the country.

In Cork, the cricket club originated in 1849 out of the newly established Queen's College. Students co-operated with those outside the college to lease the ground and members of the city's middle classes and the military provided the mainstay of its membership. In 1873 the club expanded to become the Cork and County Cricket Club. The President of the club was Sir George C. Colthurst and from then until 1954 the office was held by a member of the Colthurst family of Blarney.

The cricket grounds were designated the main sports grounds of the 1902–03 Cork International Exhibition, which attracted over 2 million people to the Mardyke area. To coincide with the Exhibition a match was organised

Cricket Field the Mardyke, Cork.

Cricket has been played at the Mardyke since 1849 (photo: Cork Public Museum)

The pavilion has been on its present site since 1879 (photo: Irish Sporting Heritage).

Richard Beamish, after whom the cricket ground is named, was a director of Beamish & Crawford, the Cork brewery which is now owned by Heineken (photo: Cork County Cricket Club).

between the Gentlemen of Ireland and London County whose side included W. G. Grace. Cork County Cricket Club provided a guarantee of £100 or the gate money. Grace is judged to have done more than any other player to popularise cricket during his long career. He famously opened for England at the age of 50, and was 51 when he played at the Mardyke ground. The International Exhibition provided the spur for the development of sports facilities in the vicinity and the clubhouse of the Sunday's Well Tennis Club was constructed to accommodate visiting dignitaries, including King Edward VII and Queen Alexandra.

During the First World War the Food Order scheme meant that the east end of the cricket ground was turned into an allotment. There were none of the traditional touring teams to compete against but cricketing activities continued against the naval and military personnel based in the area. This included an exhibition of baseball by the American Navy in 1917. With the departure of the British military in 1922 the cricket club became more dependent on local leagues, annual inter-provincials against Leinster and visits from teams such as Trinity College and Na Shulers. The Second World War also put pressure on cricket at the Mardyke as it was difficult for players to travel any great distance.

Despite the disruptions of war, cricket has survived and thrived in Cork and the pavilion at the Mardyke continues to play host to players from the national and international game.

CARLOW (RUGBY) FOOTBALL CLUB, OAK PARK

The history of Carlow Football Club reflects the development of many rugby clubs across the country. Founded in 1873, its origins were among the landed classes but long-term survival depended on extensive voluntary effort and limited funds. It sits in Oak Park, a former landed estate, which came into the hands of the Irish Land Commission in 1960. This tells its own story of the way in which sport and politics are never far apart in Ireland.

Oak Park Estate was purchased in 1775 by Henry Bruen and he was the first of five Henry Bruens to own the land. The estate consisted of about 1,600 acres enclosed within an 8ft perimeter wall. Bruen was an early patron of cricket, rugby and soccer. The last Henry Bruen died in 1954 without a male heir and the land at Oak Park was sold at auction. A British syndicate, which already owned a substantial amount of land in the area, bought the estate, infuriating local land clubs which argued that large local

estates were beyond the financial means of small farmers and that they should be bought by the Land Commission and divided into smaller portions. Things came to a head in 1960 when the head of the British syndicate, Mr G. W. Harold, received a letter containing an Irish postmark and a single bullet. This, coupled with verbal threats to his life and a poor harvest, persuaded him to contact the Land Commission to dispose of the estate. In May 1961 Carlow Golf Club purchased its current site from the Commission for a sum of £2,500.

In 1964 Carlow Football Club bought 12 acres of Oak Park from the Land Commission, ending almost 100 years of itinerancy for the club. Although its first games were played in Oak Park the club had survived for years with no fixed home. This put it under great strain and, by the late 1950s it had barely enough members to field one team and had only essential equipment – a set of touchline flags

What were once private lands are now shared facilities. The arch leading into Oak Park was the living accommodation for a gatekeeper and was occupied until the 1970s (photo: Irish Sporting Heritage).

Left: In 1972 the club purchased the jockey changing rooms from the famous Baldoyle Racecourse and moved them to Carlow (photo: Irish Sporting Heritage).

Left: The clubhouse burned down in 1987 and was rebuilt (photo: Irish Sporting Heritage).

Above: Carlow Golf Club also purchased ground from the Land Commission and took up possession in 1961. However, its first home (while it was still known as the Leinster Golf Club), was in Gotham, midway between Carlow and Maganey, and was easily reached by rail from either station. This first pavilion cost £99 and was erected in 1904 (photo: Carlow Library).

Left: In 1964 Carlow Football Club obtained 12 acres from the Land Commission and began building its own clubhouse (photo: County Carlow Football Club).

The simple box stand is common in clubs throughout the country. This stand is given a decorative touch with a faux pediment (photo: Irish Sporting Heritage).

and a pair of goalposts – with club meetings being held in different premises each season. Once the land was purchased, finances for the development of the club were raised by the organisation of dances that were held as far apart as Wexford and Drogheda. Stories of running concerts, raffles, sweeps and plays in order to raise money for facilities are familiar to clubs of all sporting codes across Ireland. The significance of these sites to their communities goes far beyond the buildings raised.

Carlow Football Club is also responsible for preserving a building from one of Ireland's premier racecourses. In 1972 it purchased at auction the Georgian-style building that had served as jockey changing rooms at Baldoyle Racecourse. A contractor agreed to take on the job of reconstruction but would not take responsibility for transporting the material from one location to another. Club members therefore undertook the task of moving the changing rooms from Baldoyle.

The corrugated iron walls and sprocket roof of Baldoyle's jockey changing rooms now sit in Oak Park, which is once again home to multiple sports, including rugby, golf, Gaelic games and soccer.

HANDBALL COURTS, COLÁISTE EINDE, GALWAY

Above: Handball alleys are a common feature of the Irish landscape. Here, viewed from the sky, and on the left-hand side of the photograph, are the large concrete alleys built at Coláiste Einde in Taylor's Hill, Galway, in the late 1920s. The alleys served the school, but also the wider handball community of Galway, Clare and Mayo (photo: Seamus Kelly).

Facing page: While Coláiste Einde continues life as a thriving school, the handball alleys are no longer used. Although they are in a good state of repair, they have become, as shown here on the left, a target for graffiti artists (photo: Irish Sporting Heritage).

Handball is one of the oldest games in Ireland. Listed as a banned activity by the Statutes of Galway in 1527, the game was originally played against the external walls of buildings such as churches and castles. Handball alleys began emerging in the eighteenth century, and the game was one of the initial sports promoted by the GAA after is foundation in 1884. With the relatively cheap availability of bricks and concrete, plus voluntary labour, many communities across Ireland were able to build an alley, and these often became the centre of parish life. With the move indoors of the game from the 1950s, many alleys have been abandoned or demolished. It is estimated that over 700 alleys remain in the country, and the Irish Handball Alley Project (www.irishhandballalley.com) has been collecting photographs of all those that still exist, even though the majority are no longer used.

Coláiste Einde came into existence in 1928, and was originally located in Furbo. In 1937, it moved to its current location in Taylor's Hill, Galway, originally working as an Irish medium preparatory boarding school. In the process of building the school, the decision was taking to build four interconnected alleys, and these would have been an important sporting outlet for the boarders in such a school. Former pupils remember playing during their morning and afternoon breaks, as well as long into the evening when perhaps they should have been focusing on evening study.

As the game of handball has moved indoors, so the alleys have been put to a variety of uses. The most original was the decision of the artist Dorothy Cross to use the Coláiste Einde alleys for the performance of her work *Chiasm* in May 1999. On the floor of the alley were projected images of a limestone tidal pool from the Aran Islands, while a tenor and soprano sang excerpts from romantic operas (photo: Dorothy Cross).

Handball alleys were a common feature of many secondary schools built in the post-independence period. They were relatively cheap to build, required minimal space (and as such were popular in many urban schools with limited land), and needed very little upkeep compared with a grass pitch. The alleys at Coláiste Einde, while a common design for a four-court alley, are unusual as most alleys contained only one or two courts. The Coláiste Einde alleys were, because of their location in the major city of the west of Ireland, used for a variety of senior competitions, and attracted star players from across Galway and Mayo. With the widening of the sporting curriculum in schools such as Coláiste Einde, and a decline in interest in the game, the handball alleys fell into disuse and were abandoned in the 1990s.

These particular alleys were given one last night in the spotlight by the acclaimed artist Dorothy Cross. In 1999, she conceived a performance piece for the handball alleys. She pre-recorded a wave sequence from the Aran Islands, which was projected on the floor of the alleys, and in adjoining alleys two performers sang a selection of operatic pieces. A key part of the rationale of the project for Cross were the handball alleys of Coláiste Einde themselves. Cross had been aware of the high number of abandoned alleys as she drove around Ireland in the 1990s. What had once been a focus for the community, a place of sporting enjoyment and play, alleys were being left to crumble and were semi-derelict markers of the past whose presence went unnoticed. Her work at Coláiste Einde, entitled *Chiasm*, was spectacular, and played to the architecture of the alleys. Now, the handball alleys of the school are carefully fenced off to avoid accidents, but are much used as a canvas for the graffiti artists of that part of Galway and the occasional lunchtime kickabout. Like many other alleys around the country, those at Coláiste Einde, which would have been the sporting focus for generations of schoolboys, have an uncertain future. It is doubtful that they will ever be used for handball again, and it is unlikely that a school, which, like all others, has to carefully manage its budget, will pay the upkeep on a largely unused structure.

LAHINCH GOLF CLUB, CLARE

Lahinch Golf Club was founded in 1892 on a course that had been laid out by the Black Watch Regiment (photo: National Library of Ireland).

The golf course at Lahinch was opened in 1892 and it not only changed the local landscape but transformed the local economy by bringing affluent visitors to the area. Its history combines all the significant elements for the development of golf in the nineteenth century: railways, the military and tourists.

Typical of golf courses constructed in the nineteenth century, Lahinch was built within a short distance of the railway line. The West Clare Railway had been opened between Ennis and Kilrush in 1887. The Golfing Union of Ireland, formed in 1881, had set out with the aim of working with railway companies to obtain better facilities for golfers and the Great Southern and Western Railway provided a special golfing rate for those travelling from Dublin to Ennis. Members of golf clubs were drawn largely from the professional and middle classes and clubs often had strong links to the British Army – the course at Lahinch was laid out by members of the Black Watch Regiment. Many clubs noticed a considerable drop in membership during the years of the Anglo-Boer War, (1899–1901) and during the First World War.

John Burke, the legendary Lahinch golfer, indicated the change to the locality brought about by the arrival of golf. He remembered the first day of golf in the town on 15 April 1892: 'Four horses clothed in white foam made a dramatic entrance as they thundered through the Main

The West Clare Railway, seen here, opened in 1887, making it possible to build a golf course and hotel, also in the photo, in an otherwise remote part of Ireland (photo: National Library of Ireland).

Street . . . It was the first time the locals saw a coachman and four in hand. It was Good Friday and one local remarked: "Glory be to God I hear they are going to eat meet on this blessed day. What's the world coming to at all!" Before the game of golf began, the flags were hoisted and toasts were drunk to His Majesty the King.'

In order to cater for travellers, railway companies constructed impressive hotels at key tourist destinations across Ireland, such as the Great Southern Hotel in Killarney and the Great Northern Hotel in Bundoran. Members of the golf club at Lahinch realised the importance of providing accommodation for visitors and decided to raise the finances for a luxury golf hotel. Before it was built there had only been one hostelry in Lahinch. The Golf Hotel opened its doors in 1896 and was built in the Swiss style, of pitch pine with a fashionable and luxurious interior. The hotel thrived, providing accommodation for distinguished guests from Ireland and Britain in the period before the First World War. Its popularity declined in the 1920s and, in March 1933, the hotel burned down.

Within a few years of opening, Lahinch Golf Club had established a first-class course. It employed the services of Old Tom Morris (the most famous green-keeper of his day) to make improvements to the layout in 1894 and, in the following year, the inaugural South of Ireland Golf Championship was held at the club. This is the oldest of the Irish provincial championships and has been held continuously, except for the period of the First World War and in 1922 because of the Irish Civil War. In 1927 Dr Alister MacKenzie, a well-known golf architect, also added improvements to the course.

Sport and railways linked remote parts of Ireland to larger patterns of commercial development so that formal competitions and professionally designed courses attracted tourists and created significant economic hubs across the country.

The luxury golf hotel at Lahinch opened its doors in 1896. The hotel stood three storeys high with an iron roof and stone basement. The rooms, which provided accommodation for forty people, had balconies and sanitary appliances 'of the most approved description' (photo: National Library of Ireland).

Above: A new clubhouse was built in 1947 and has been constantly updated and refurbished (photo: Damien Murphy).

Left: The remains of Dough Castle can still be found on the seventh hole of the Castle Course. The castle was originally founded by the O'Connors in 1306. The surrounding sandhills are said to be the haunt of Donn Dumhach, the Fairy King, and the sandhill Crughaneer near the bridge is also said to be haunted (photo: Lahinch Golf Club).

THE MARKETS FIELD, LIMERICK

Sport was first played in the Markets Field in 1886 when an athletics event was held there and a rich variety of sports has taken place there ever since. This photo shows a Garda sports day in 1929 (Irish Sporting Heritage).

The Markets Field has played a central role in the story of sport in Limerick since the 1880s. Architecturally the venue has little to recommend it but the threat of closure in 1974 prompted the local media to characterise it as 'Limerick's oldest and most popular venue'. As one of Ireland's great multi-purpose grounds, the Markets Field has been home to athletics, Gaelic games, rugby, soccer, greyhound racing, Garda sports, as well as carnivals, circuses and wrestling contests. It has held political meetings and was used by the British Army to mobilise for

the First World War. However, the drive to modernise and to cater for the expectations of spectators meant that its future seemed uncertain.

Sport was first played in the Markets Field (which was owned by a business consortium) in 1886 when the Irish Cycling Association and the Gaelic Athletic Association paid £8 a day to organise athletics events over the course of three consecutive Sundays. In the following decade the Markets Field established itself as an important venue and, in 1896, the Limerick county senior hurling championship

Greyhound racing first came to the Markets Field in 1932 and remained until 2010 (photo: Irish Greyhound Board).

The drive to modernise and to cater for the expectations of customers had led to the relocation of greyhound racing from Market's Field, shown here, to a new stadium on the site of the old Limerick Racecourse, which was host to the visits to Ireland of Pope John Paul II and John F. Kennedy, and the World Championship Cross Country victory of John Treacy (photo: Irish Greyhound Board).

final was played there between Caherline and Ballingarry. Rugby was also played in the venue which was home to the famous Garryowen club, which gave its name to the 'up and under' kick and became a byword for Limerick across the world.

In Limerick, rugby has been played by a more diverse demographic than in the rest of Ireland since its origins. Skilled artisans were encouraged to join local clubs at the end of the nineteenth century and rugby has had a strong base among the county's working class population ever since. This has given Limerick rugby a very strong sense of its own identity and the Markets Field has played an important part in this story. In 1906 the grounds hosted an international between Munster and the All Blacks. The crushing defeat of the home side meant that it is not the best remembered of New Zealand's trips to Limerick.

The pressures on multi-purpose grounds such as the Markets Field were considerable as the pitch had little time to recover between events. By the 1920s complaints were constant from players and spectators about the poor condition of the playing surface. Sporting bodies therefore endeavoured to build their own grounds in order to have more control over the quality and use of facilities. In 1928 the GAA in Limerick moved to the Gaelic Grounds on the Ennis Road and had ceased to play any matches in the Markets Field by 1932. In 1931 the Munster Branch of the IRFU decided to acquire land to be used exclusively for rugby and purchased 7½ acres at Hassetts Cross for £1,130 on what was to become known as Thomond Park. Rugby continued to be played at the Markets Field at club level until Garryowen sold out their rights and moved to Dooradoyle in 1957.

When rugby and Gaelic games had departed from the Markets Field, greyhound racing and soccer made their homes there. Greyhound racing spread rapidly through Ireland in the 1930s and arrived in the Markets Field in 1932. Part of its success was due to the fact that it could be set up in existing soccer and rugby pitches and did not have to acquire and equip completely new venues. Greyhound racing thrived in a multi-sport environment. Limerick has a long tradition of dog breeding and coursing and, when Bord na gCon was established as a semi-state body in 1958, it settled in the city. The Markets Field staged the Irish Derby in 1939, the Irish Oaks in 1944 and hosted the Irish St Ledger from 1944. Pressure to provide more modern facilities for customers meant that Bord na gCon moved to a new stadium in 2010, on the site of the old Limerick Racecourse.

Despite the multitude of sports that have been played there, many Limerick soccer fans consider the Markets Field to be their spiritual home. Limerick AFC was founded in 1934 and (through several guises) made the Markets Field its base until 1984 when it left in a move that was extremely unpopular with supporters who have long campaigned for a return to the venue. In 2011 the Charitable Foundation of the businessman J. P. McManus purchased the ground from Bord na gCon for €1.5 million, and from 2012 it will once again be the home of Limerick soccer.

FITZWILLIAM TENNIS CLUB, DUBLIN

Founded in 1877, the Fitzwilliam Tennis Club is one of the oldest tennis clubs in Ireland. It derived its name from the first courts it leased, just off Fitzwilliam Square. Pictured here is the clubhouse that was built during the Club's occupancy of its grounds on Wilton Place. The clubhouse was built by a Mr Metz of London, who was an importer of Norwegian and Swedish houses, and this is reflected in the look of the building (photo: Fitzwilliam Tennis Club).

The Dublin Lawn Tennis Club was formed in November 1877, and at a subsequent meeting the decision was made to lease a patch of open ground in Upper Pembroke Street, just off Fitzwilliam Square, on which to build courts for the club. In December that same year, it was decided to rename the club the 'Fitzwilliam'. An early report of a club match, against the University Club in 1880, noted how the game was played in front of 'a large and fashionable assembly', in 'weather that was all that could be desired, and everything tended to make the match enjoyable and a

perfect success'. As tennis was such a popular sport among Dublin's middle and upper classes in the late Victorian years, the original premises were deemed too small. A ground was found at Wilton Place where courts could be constructed, and 6 Wilton Place was purchased for use as a premises for the administration of the club.

The building of the Wilton Place facilities began in earnest in 1902, when a Mr Metz was contracted to construct a clubhouse. As an importer of Swedish and Norwegian houses, it was perhaps unsurprising that Metz's

Above: In 1969, the Fitzwilliam Club decided to move to a new site off Appian Way and their current facilities were completed in the early 1970s. These have been updated on a regular basis ever since, and it is the premier facility in Ireland (photo: Damien Murphy).

Facing page: Pictured here, the buildings of the Fitzwilliam Club not only feature the usual bars and rooms of a clubhouse, but include an indoor tennis facility and squash courts. Note the use of large amounts of roof glass, to the right of the photo, allowing daylight to illuminate the court (photo: Damien Murphy).

design is remembered by many older members of the club as looking like a Swedish summerhouse, an architectural oddity in suburban Dublin. In 1969, the facilities at Wilton Place were ageing, and the decision was made for the club to move again. This time it secured its current property on Appian Way, and opened its doors in 1971. It was the most modern tennis facility in Ireland. When the new facility opened, the newspapers were fulsome in their praise: 'the most comprehensive (and at £0.25 million the most expensive) sporting complex in the country, the new Fitzwilliam lawn tennis club is having its international christening this week, as the Irish Open championships are being staged there for the first time.' The facility was designed by Stephenson Gibney and Associates, and covered a 4½- acre site. It originally included seven outdoor hard courts, two indoor courts, four grass courts, six squash courts, a running track, a swimming pool and sauna. According to the architects, the buildings at the club were designed to evoke the Edwardian period, and this was achieved through the extensive use of sculptured brickwork. Given that the Fitzwilliam was the most

frequent venue for tournament tennis in Ireland, its centre court was designed with seating for 3,000, and an open terrace on the clubhouse roof could seat 500 people. For all the modernity of the new facilities, *The Irish Times* noted, 'in these days of libertarian feminism, Fitzwilliam is an all male club, and ladies are only allowed in under rigorous conditions'. By 1975, the men-only rule was attracting the attentions of campaigning feminists, and in July that year, thirty members of Irish Women United invaded the club, chanting, amongst other things, 'who's afraid of Virginia Wade?' In 1996, the club voted to change its rules and admit women members.

The club itself has continued to develop its facilities, and now comprises five outdoor artificial grass courts, four indoor courts, two clay courts, six squash courts, a gym, swimming pool and snooker room. It remains one of the premier tennis clubs in Ireland, and while the heyday of Irish Open tennis has passed, in terms of spectator popularity, the Fitzwilliam remains the location of the Open tournament, which it has hosted since 1879.

RAILWAY UNION BOWLS CLUB, DUBLIN

Bowls of one form or another have been played in Ireland since the eighteenth century. The earliest greens were in Dublin at Great Marlborough Street, at Trinity College and in Chapelizod, but all these seem to have been developed for other uses as Dublin grew, and by the early nineteenth century bowls appears to have disappeared from the city's pleasures. In 1892, Dublin's first modern bowls club came together at the home of Charles Eason, the bookseller, in Kenilworth Square. The membership made this a very exclusive club, as they were drawn from Eason's business partners and neighbours. The first games were actually played on Eason's lawns, before moving into Kenilworth Square, and then in 1909 onto a purpose-laid green in Grosvenor Square. From the Kenilworth club, an enthusiasm for bowls spread across Dublin (the first club

outside the capital was formed in Cork in 1912) and was particularly notable amongst workplace sports clubs (the Imperial Tobacco club and the St James's Gate club were both formed prior to the First World War).

The Railway and Steampacket Company Irish Athletic and Social Union was formed at a meeting at the Rotunda on Parnell Square in March 1905. The founding aim of the club was to promote 'social intercourse fostering manly sports amongst the clerical and professional staffs of the various railway and shipping companies in Dublin'. With the backing of the companies involved, the club was able to purchase grounds at Park Avenue, Sydney Parade, and pitches were laid out for the various sports that the union supported. On 25 April 1907, at the clubhouse on Park Avenue the decision was taken to form a bowls club. By

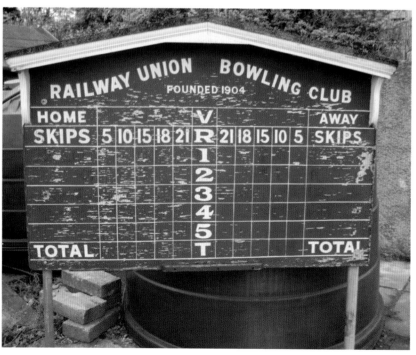

Left: The scoreboard at the Railway Union, weathered by time, proudly declares the date of foundation, which makes this club one of the oldest in Ireland (photo: Irish Sporting Heritage).

Facing page:
Main photograph: The Railway Union Bowls clubhouse is shown here between the two flag poles. The clubhouse is now flanked, on the left, by the larger and more recent clubhouse of the Bank of Ireland (photo: Irish Sporting Heritage).
Inset: Based in Sandymount, the Railway Union Bowls club was founded in 1904, and is part of the larger multi-sport Railway Union sports club. It is one of a number of sports clubs in south Dublin, which has one of the largest concentrations of sporting clubs in the world (photo: Irish Sporting Heritage).

the following summer the new bowling green was unveiled and the first club championship played there. In the inaugural tournament, thirty-two bowlers took part and the final was played between Mr Mounsey (LNWR) and Mr Berkeley (GNRI), with the former taking the trophy.

In 1911, at the seventh annual meeting of the Union, it was recorded that the club supported teams in football, rugby, hockey, tennis, bowls and cricket, and that there were 396 members. Importantly, for the long-term success of the Union, it was noted that the financial position of the Union was 'better than ever'. It is also clear from the list of those who attended the meeting that this was not simply a sporting club for the railway workers, but rather one that was backed at the highest level, with twelve of the railway and shipping companies sending representatives to the meeting. This support was invaluable in getting the

Railway Union into its own grounds so quickly, supporting the growth of its games and, in the context of bowls, getting a green laid within a year of formation. The strength of Railway Union bowls was evidenced in 1927, when it became one of the five founder members of the Bowling League of Ireland and also the Irish Bowling Association, which would be responsible for the administration of the game in the country.

With the demise of the plethora of private railway companies, the Railway Union continued as a members' sport club, and its bowls section has been a permanent feature of the club. It still plays on the same site, and still competes in the Bowling League of Ireland, which has expanded its geographical spread of member clubs over the last two decades.

BLACKROCK AND DUN LAOGHAIRE BATHS, DUBLIN

The Dun Laoghaire Baths, or the Royal Victorian Baths as they were originally called, were built in 1843. They were bought by the local council in the1890s, and became a cornerstone of the town's attractions for day trippers from Dublin. By the mid-1930s, the baths included three pools, a tea room, laundry and a lounge, as well as a range of indoor medicinal baths. The proximity of the baths to the railway station enhanced their popularity (photo: Dublin City Libraries).

In 1997, plans were put in place to replace the Dun Laoghaire baths with a major water park. The plans came to nothing, and the baths were closed. Since then they have become derelict (photo: Damien Murphy).

Right: The Liffey Swim began in 1920 with an opening field of twenty-seven men. The event grew steadily, reaching its peak in the 1950s. Women were allowed to enter the swim from 1991, and the event is still held annually on a late summer Saturday (photo: Dublin City Libraries).

Below: Blackrock baths were built by the railway company next to the tracks in 1839, five years after the Dublin–Kingstown line had first opened. Tickets could be purchased in Dublin that covered the cost of the rail journey as well as entrance to the baths. In 1877, the baths were modernised to include the large concrete pool, and in 1928 ownership passed to the local council (photo: Dublin City Libraries).

Irish Amateur Swimming Association
(LEINSTER BRANCH)

PROGRAMME
OF
SECOND ANNUAL

LIFFEY RACE
FOR
THE CHALLENGE CUP
(Presented by the "Irish Independent")

WEDNESDAY, 10TH AUGUST, 1921
STARTING AT 6 P.M.

PRICE THREEPENCE

For an island, and one blessed with a network of lakes and rivers, it is perhaps unsurprising that nature has been harnessed to allow the Irish to swim. In the nineteenth century, with concerns over health and fitness, it is fair to say that a swimming craze began. Across the country, outdoor pools and lidos were built and then, into the twentieth century, indoor facilities were added. The 1846 Baths and Wash Houses Act ushered in a wealth of public bathing and swimming amenities in Britain and, although the Act applied to Ireland, fewer facilities were built here. Even in Belfast, the public provision of baths was slow in coming. The Templemore Public Baths, which cost £21,000 to build and which are still in use today, did not open for business until 1893. They were built by the City Corporation, and were designed to provide cleanliness for the East Belfast population, as well as introducing them to the health-giving qualities of swimming. When opened, the Baths boasted two bathing spaces for washing and two pools for recreational and competitive swimming. In Dublin, the most opulent baths were opened in 1905. The Iveagh Trust Baths were provided for the population around Christchurch, and were part of a plan to clean up the slums in that part of the city. Designed by the London firm of Joseph, Smitherm and Joseph, the Baths are one of Dublin's finest examples of an art nouveau building. In the 1990s, the building was redesigned as a fitness club, and while much of the internal space was remodelled, the exterior was left untouched and the pool is of the same design as the original.

For all the comforts provided by late-nineteenth- and early-twentieth-century indoor pools, these were, until the 1960s, the exception rather than the rule. For most Irish people who wished to swim, they relied on outdoor pools that were usually built on the coast to cater for urban dwellers or tourists. The two most iconic, certainly in the Dublin area, were the baths at Blackrock and Dun Laoghaire.

Billy Morrison was an Irish swimming and high-diving champion. He was a regular at Blackrock Baths in the 1950s and his acrobatic skills from the high board drew many admirers (photo: Dublin City Libraries).

Blackrock Baths were built in 1839 beside the railway station and were paid for by the railway company. In 1887, the baths were expanded to include a large concrete gentlemen's pool, and a smaller ladies' pool. Despite the expansion, the water that fed the pools was initially drawn from the sea, and swimmers complained of the amounts of seaweed that found its way into the pools. Works were undertaken to cure this problem and in 1880 *The Irish Times* was able to report: 'the public will be glad to learn that new arrangements have been made by which these really splendid baths are supplied with pure water and the

Above: In the 1950s and 1960s, the popularity of outdoor swimming waned as the first indoor pools were built in Dublin. Due to rising costs and falling attendances, the local council made the decision to close the baths. They remain derelict, and while there have been campaigns mounted to redevelop the baths, there are no firm plans at present for the site (photo: Damien Murphy).

seaweed practically excluded . . . in addition to the splendid basin filled with water as clear as crystal, these baths possess an advantage peculiar to themselves in combining with it fine open sea bathing, and should form one of the greatest of the rapidly increasing attractions of Blackrock.' While a place of pleasure, the Blackrock Baths were also used for competitive swimming and in 1928 hosted the swimming events that were part of that year's Tailteann Games. The pool area also included seating for up to 1,000 spectators. In the same year as the Games, the Urban District Council bought the baths, and they became a publicly owned amenity. The baths were hugely popular in the 1940s and 1950s, but began to decline from the 1960s when greater numbers of indoor pools were built across Dublin. In the late 1980s, the baths were closed and in 1992 much of the site was dismantled. The derelict remains of Blackrock's great attraction can still be seen next to the DART station.

Further down the coast, the first pool at Dun Laoghaire was built in the 1790s, but was later removed to make way for the railway line connecting what was then Kingstown, with Dublin. In 1843, the Royal Victorian Baths opened, and included bathing facilities, and both freshwater and seawater swimming pools. This was not simply a place of public bathing, but rather an attraction for the people of

Dublin that allowed them to access health-giving baths and treatments, to swim and also to take tea in the famed tea room, which was also open to non-bathers. In 1910 the baths were remodelled by the local council. As with Blackrock, the baths remained popular through to the 1960s, but rather than lose custom to those seeking indoor swimming, Dun Laoghaire opened its indoor pools and water fun park, named Rainbow Rapids, in the 1970s. In 1997, in the face of falling customer numbers and the high cost of maintaining what was essentially a Victorian site with modern additions, the decision was made to close the baths. Since then there has been a long-running local campaign to redevelop the site, with swimming at its heart, and in 2008, a €125 million plan was put before the local council to redevelop the town's seafront. This plan has advanced no further, given prevailing economic conditions, and the baths remain derelict.

Swimming, then, has been at the heart of Irish sporting life. The many pools that were built around the country in the late nineteenth century captured the athletic spirit of the time, but most have fallen into disuse. Ireland still has, compared to most European countries, a low provision of public swimming facilities, and what dominates are pools situated in private health clubs and spas.

BELVEDERE HUNTING LODGE, WESTMEATH

Belvedere was built in 1740 as a hunting and fishing lodge. Westmeath County Council bought the estate, including Mullingar Golf Club, in 1982 for IR£250,000 (photo: Belvedere House).

Above: Hunting in Westmeath dates from the end of the seventeenth century and the Westmeath Hunt was established in 1854. It was the first hunt to be organised by subscription (photo: Westmeath County Library).

Left: Hunting continues as a popular sport in Ireland and, because of a ban on fox hunting in Britain, attracts enthusiasts from across the Irish Sea (photo: Sarah English).

Facing page: Hunting was central to the social and economic life of the landed gentry in Ireland. This photograph shows the opening of the Waterford Hunt in October 1900 (photo: National Library of Ireland).

Belvedere was built in 1740 as a fishing and hunting lodge. It was built by Robert Rochfort, the first Baron Belfield, who was later to take the title Lord Belvedere. The architect Richard Castle was one of the leading architects of his day and Belvedere ranks as one of his most accomplished designs. The house has the finest rococo ceilings in Ireland and the largest and most spectacular folly in the country: the Jealous Wall. It is now in public ownership and operates as a museum. It is an example of the way in which the site of an elite sport has been reconfigured as national heritage.

Hunting in Westmeath dates from the end of the seventeenth century and over the following 200 years it became central to the social and cultural lives of upper class society. Hunting also provided British army officers, who were drawn primarily from the landed classes, with a seamless introduction into local upper class society, and influential political, legal and financial networks were maintained between the civilian and military communities. Most hunts met twice a week (prestigious ones like Kildare's met seven days per week) and the total number of hunts in the country averaged around 150 a week during the eight-month hunting season. It was estimated that the sport involved an annual expenditure of £500,000 and was therefore crucial to the rural economy. The highlight of the social calendar was the annual Hunt Ball. The first ball for the Westmeath Hunt was held in Ballinlough Castle in 1861 and the first one to be held in Westmeath was at Knockdrin Castle in 1866.

The Great Famine had a devastating impact on Irish rural life and sections of the landed gentry were ruined by it. In response to the changed circumstances, hunting became organised by subscription in order to share the financial burden of maintaining the pack. In 1854 Sir Richard Levinge issued a notice to landowners in Westmeath that a pack of foxhounds had been purchased,

and within a few weeks a committee was established and a subscription of £600 was raised from forty-two individuals. The formation of the Westmeath Hunt Club radically altered the way in which hunting was organised as the cost was more widely distributed. There is no direct evidence of Belvedere hosting the Westmeath Hunt but it was clearly an integral part of the sporting and social life of the area.

During the land agitation of the 1880s the hunt became a target for Land Leaguers and meets could not be publicised. Small sealed cards were posted to members of the hunt in order to maintain secrecy. The largest demonstration in Westmeath was at Lisnabin in 1881 at which 200 protestors gathered to disrupt the hunt. No one was seriously injured. The highest-profile hunting casualty of the land agitation was the long-established Curraghmore Hunt, which ceased to exist after an attack by a 300-strong crowd. Steeplechase meetings were still strongly linked to hunting and there was a fear that they would not survive in Leinster, such was the pressure on the hunt. The Kildare Hunt was forced to call off the Punchestown Races in 1882 (these were again abandoned during the War of Independence under pressure from Sinn Féin).

Belvedere House was acquired by Westmeath County Council in 1982. Prior to this it had a series of eccentric owners, including Robert Rochfort who was known as the 'Wicked Earl' because he kept his wife effectively under house arrest for thirty-one years until his death in 1774, and Colonel Charles Kenneth Howard-Bury who led the Everest Reconnaissance mission with Mallory in 1921 and was responsible for introducing the idea of the yeti to Europe. Belvedere was opened to the public in 2000 after an extensive refurbishment costing IR£5.7 million was undertaken by the Council and the Irish Tourist Board. The stable yard and parts of the basement and ground floor of the house have been developed as an interpretative centre.

DOWN ROYAL RACECOURSE, DOWN

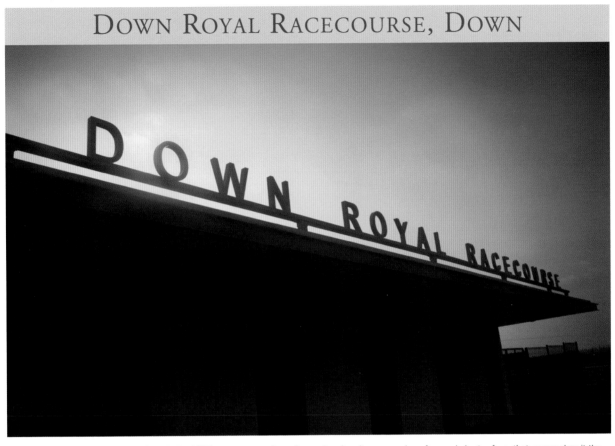

The Down Royal Corporation was founded in 1685 to encourage breeding and racing. Its possession of a royal charter from that year makes it the oldest racing institution in the country (photo: Peter Higgins).

The Down Royal Corporation of Horsebreeders was created in 1685 by Royal Charter from King James II, with the objective of encouraging horse breeding in the county. Down Royal is the oldest racing institution in Ireland.

Horse racing in Ireland had long preceded the establishment of the Down Royal Corporation but this marked the beginning of its formal organisation. Horses had come to be seen more explicitly as commodities that could be traded and raced and so institutions were established to set standards for stallions and oversee the running of race meetings and horse fairs.

The first racecourse of the Down Royal Corporation was a three-mile, undulating horseshoe shape at Downpatrick. Racing moved to the Maze, where it continues, in the early eighteenth century. The site had been set aside by Arthur Hill who resided in Hillsborough

Vendors with tents, booths and sideshows were part of the general spectacle and excitement of race meetings. This photograph shows Toft's Show on Tramore Amusement Field during the Tramore Races in 1901. Such amusements would have been familiar at race courses across the country at the time (photo: National Library of Ireland).

Castle. Hill had the ear of the King and, in June 1690, when William III was at Hillsborough on his way to the Battle of the Boyne, Hill informed the King that Down Royal had not been subsidised by royal grant. The King immediately sent an autographed letter to Christopher Carlton, the Collector of Customs in Belfast, granting £100 for a King's Plate to be raced for annually. The Byerley Turk, one of the three foundation sires of modern thoroughbred racing (all modern thoroughbreds descend from one of these stallions), won the 'Silver Bell' in Down Royal in 1690, while on the way to the Boyne where he joined the Williamite armies as a charger.

In 1750, King George II donated another £100 and from then to the present day a Royal Plate has been held at Down Royal that is contributed to by the Privy Purse. The King's Plates were the highlight of eighteenth-century racing and were confined to Irish-bred horses and run under strict rules, again in order to improve horse breeding and commerce. In the nineteenth century the number of Royal Plates increased and were extended beyond Down Royal and the Curragh, and continued to constitute the principle prizes in Irish racing.

Entries in the racing calendar show many fewer races in Ulster than in the other three provinces. Opposition to gambling among Presbyterians and some members of the Church of Ireland meant that racing was not as widespread across the North. Down Royal was undoubtedly the primary northern horse racing venue and special trains took race-goers from the Curragh railway siding and Amiens Street Station in Dublin for race meetings. Free carriage was also provided for horses from Dublin to the Maze.

The cream of Ulster society gathered for the Down Royal races and, in early July 1916, the races were abandoned in the wake of the news of the devastating number of casualties on the opening days of the Battle of the Somme. The race meeting took place instead a month later. It was noted that significant numbers had travelled from Dublin and across the Irish Channel, which led to large crowds in the public stands. The reserved stands at Down Royal, however, were sparsely populated due to 'so many of the principal Ulster families being in mourning'. Racing fixtures were circumscribed during the First World War but Down Royal was one of the courses sanctioned by the War Cabinet and therefore continued for the duration of the War. The year 1922 was a difficult one for racing and many meetings were cancelled. In July, meetings at Baldoyle, Tuam and Down Royal were all abandoned, and in August 1922 the second day's racing at the Maze was cancelled 'owing to the funeral of Michael Collins taking place on that day, and out of sympathy'.

No racing took place at Down Royal between 1940

and 1946 because of the Second World War but the course immediately established itself as a significant part of the Irish racing calendar in the years after the War. Since the early 1990s the racecourse has undertaken major development and modernisation. The Ulster Derby is the highlight of its three-day summer festival and the Northern Ireland Festival of Racing in early November is a showcase for National Hunt (jump) racing

After major redevelopment since 1993, Down Royal has been in a constant state of redevelopment and modernisation (photo: Peter Higgins).

Hosting twelve race meetings per year, including the Ulster Derby, Down Royal is one of only two racecourses in the north of Ireland (photo: Peter Higgins)

GARDA ROWING CLUB, DUBLIN

Competitive rowing in Ireland was popular in the nineteenth century and at that time, was centred on the River Liffey around Ringsend. For many of the wealthy social classes involved in rowing, the Liffey had two problems. Firstly, it was a busy entrance to the quays of Dublin city and, at the time, heavily polluted, and secondly, the sport attracted many working class rowers who worked on the river professionally and, to the minds of the elite, corrupted the gentlemanly ethos of the sport. The answer to these problems was to move. One of the oldest rowing clubs in Ireland, the Dublin University Boat Club was the first to move. Established in 1836, originally as the Pembroke Club and rowing from Ringsend, the club made itself socially exclusive when, in 1847, it restricted its membership to those gentlemen who had ties to Trinity College. In 1898, the club left Ringsend, and moved across the city to Islandbridge. Here the Liffey was ideal for rowing and without the working traffic and debris associated with the city centre location. The club was the first to build a boathouse at Islandbridge, and also worked on the river itself, to improve it rowing conditions, and straightened and widened what is now the enclosure stretch.

After the University Club relocated, others followed and any new clubs that were founded in Dublin, such as the Neptune Club in 1908, chose to locate themselves at Islandbridge. The clubs were a mix of those formed around institutions, such as the University Club and the Commercial Club (originally formed in 1856 for the traders and professionals of Henry Street and Grafton Street), or else comprised rowing enthusiasts with no common bond beyond their love of the sport. On the institutional side, the Dublin Metropolitan Police had been active in regattas in the late nineteenth century and, after

the foundation of the state the Garda Síochána began rowing, particularly in Wexford.

Throughout the 1920s, interest in rowing grew amongst the Gardaí, and in 1931 the Garda Síochána Boat Club affiliated with the Irish Amateur Rowing Union. That same year the inaugural internal rowing competition took place at Islandbridge. By the mid-1930s, the club had moved to Islandbridge, but from what records are available, it appears that they only had the most basic of facilities. In 1943, the Garda Síochána Benevolent Society approved a grant of £650 to the boat club to allow it to build a boat wharf and four tennis courts on lands, amounting to 2 acres at Islandbridge, that the club was aiming to lease. In 1954 the boat club was formally opened at its Islandbridge site, alongside the Garda Pitch and Putt, and Tennis clubs, which shared the river front site. Two boats were ordered from Hickey's boatbuilders in Galway, and for the first few years the club stored these in the boathouse of the Commercial Club.

In 1960 a modern boathouse for the club was opened by Garda Commissioner Daniel Costigan, and blessed by Father Gill. The boathouse was designed by Dermot J. Farrelly, and housed sliding racks for storing boats (the first time such racks had been installed in Ireland), as well as meeting spaces for members. In 2004, the boathouse was updated and remodelled. The building cost €1.3 million, and included a new boat storage space and gymnasium. This building of the new boathouse was a means, in part, of celebrating the fiftieth anniversary of the foundation of the club, its excellent facilities fitting for a club that has produced so many national and international champions. The club is significant as it still serves the rowing enthusiasms of a membership whose day job is to police the streets of Ireland.

Members of the Garda Síochána had successfully rowed since the foundation of the state, and found a home in Islandbridge, where most Dublin rowing clubs were located in the late 1930s. The Club was formally founded in 1954, but borrowed the slipways and boathouses of the Neptune and Commercial Clubs (photo: Damien Murphy).

Right: The Garda club has competed around the world and won many championships. While its crews and symbols were well known by the late 1950s, the lack of a clubhouse was becoming a concern, with Con Flannery, the Honourable Secretary, stating in 1955: 'a boat club without a clubhouse is like a lighthouse without a light' (photo: Damien Murphy).

The first purpose-built Garda boathouse was opened in 1960 and was a basic concrete structure. It has been updated and remodelled on a number of occasions since, and is now one of the most modern boathouses on the Liffey (photo: Damien Murphy).

GARDA SÍOCHANA
BOAT CLUB

ROAD BOWLING, ARMAGH AND CORK

For most sporting clubs and societies the drive to build permanent facilities for the playing of games has been a crucial aspect of their development. The failure to participate in this development meant that some sports were rendered almost invisible. An emphasis on the built heritage is often weighted in favour of wealthy sports. Drag hunting, hare coursing, and skittles have not bequeathed an extensive built legacy but are nevertheless an important part of Ireland's sporting life.

Road bowling is perhaps the best known minority sport in Ireland. It is played on public roads rather than permanent courses and this means that its physical legacy is difficult to chart. However, in those counties where it is still played, it is a vital part of the sporting heritage. As a sport, road bowling is not peculiar to Ireland but it is often seen to be rooted in the landscape and as echoing simpler times. Known as 'Long Bullets', it was played extensively in Europe and America in the eighteenth century. Like many sports in Ireland it entered the country through Ulster, brought in by weavers from England and Scotland. The simplicity of its form – needing no facilities – meant that it was particularly popular among labourers and

Road bowling retains the simplicity of early sporting contests: a physical contest between two or more players. Here, David Murphy throws at the 2008 senior final at Marsh Road, Skibbereen (photo: Denis McGarry, supplied by The Irish Road Bowling Association).

A rock wall provides the perfect vantage point from which to watch road bowling in the 1950s (photo: Getty Images)

Young boys enjoy a game of road bowling on an Irish country lane in January 1955 (photo: Getty Images).

tradesmen. Although once played throughout Ireland it is now largely confined to the counties of Armagh and Cork.

The object of the game is for one of two players to cover the course (a country road) with the least number of throws of a 28 oz iron bowl. Skill and tactical play are used to negotiate a distance which can vary but which is now often 4 km in length. Several thousand spectators gather to watch important matches. Gambling is prevalent around the game and competitors can meet for high stakes.

In many ways road bowling is a sport that was antipathetic to modernisation. While most sports have benefited from urbanisation and increased motor transport, road bowling has at times been hampered by them. Increased road traffic meant that the sport died out in some areas. At the end of the nineteenth century attempts by the Royal Irish Constabulary to stop road bowling, because it took place on public roads, meant that it became a somewhat underground sport which was associated with the cultural resistance element of Irish nationalism. Its unadorned style also led the GAA to characterise it as a Gaelic sport in 1884.

Following the partition of Ireland, road bowling continued to be treated with some hostility by police forces in Northern Ireland and it was not until the 1950s that it achieved some degree of acceptance. It is also true that improved rail and road networks increased the possibilities of games being played between as well as within counties and the creation of Ból Chumann na hÉireann in 1954 has helped to regulate and promote the sport, and it organised the first All-Ireland Senior Championships (confined to Cork in its initial years) the following year. The first roads on which the championship took place were the Enniskeane, Macroom, Derrinsafa and Kilcrea Roads in Cork. In 1963 the first ever All-Ireland Final took place between Cork and Armagh on the Moy Road in Armagh.

Carmel Ryan throws in the senior ladies' All-Ireland Final in Keady, County Armagh (photo: Gretta Cormican).

The European Championship event in Bandon in May 2008 (photo: Denis McGarry, supplied by The Irish Road Bowling Association).

ROYAL ST GEORGE YACHT CLUB,
DUN LAOGHAIRE

Founded in 1838, and securing land within Kingstown Harbour from the Commissioner of Public Works, the Royal St George Yacht Club began work on its first clubhouse in 1843. Designed by Mulvany, the clubhouse was built in a neo-classical style. Here it is shown in the late nineteenth century, with a commercial ship moored on the pier to the right (photo: National Library of Ireland).

The decision to build a harbour at Kingstown, now Dun Laogahire, was made in 1815 after a storm killed 400 people in 1807. Construction, under the guidance of John Rennie and later his son, took until the 1840 before the pier was complete, and in 1842 a lighthouse was added. With a harbour opening of 750 feet, two piers, each over 4,000 feet, and an enclosed area of 251 acres of water, many believed that the Kingstown harbour was one of the finest anywhere in the British Empire. The opening of the Dublin-to-Kingstown railway in 1834 meant that the harbour was connected to the city in the most modern fashion, and it became the most important passenger, mail and freight harbour for crossings to Britain.

Shortly after the railway had been completed, and prior to the final completion of the harbour, a group of sailing enthusiasts approached the Commissioner of Public Works and asked that they be granted land on the harbour site for the construction of a club house. The sailors had previously sailed on the Liffey, but felt that conditions there were not

suitable for the leisurely pursuit. Originally named the Kingstown Boat Club when founded in 1838, it became the Royal St George Yacht Club in 1847 after being conferred the royal privileges by Queen Victoria.

While Kingstown harbour in the mid-nineteenth century was a busy working port, yachting and sailing were becoming highly popular as leisure pursuits amongst those who had the necessary means. Alongside the Royal St George Yacht Club on the harbour front were also founded the Royal Irish Yacht Club (1831) and the Kingstown Royal Harbour Boat Club (1870). As an exclusive club, the Royal St George was not simply looking for a place to play and sail: rather, it had the means to construct an impressive clubhouse and range of facilities.

Although not the oldest club in Kingstown, the Royal St George was the first to build a fit-for-purpose clubhouse on the harbour front. The original clubhouse was designed by John Skipton Mulvany, and completed between 1842 and 1843. Mulvany had been the architect appointed to

While the clubhouse has been extended a number of times, the front façade, which was built by the famed mid-nineteenth-century Dublin builder Masterson, has remained largely untouched (photo: Royal St George Yacht Club).

the original Dublin-to-Kingstown railway, and knew the harbour front well. He was a well-regarded architect of the period, and was also responsible for the railway stations at Galway and Athlone, and in Dublin the station at Broadstone. By 1845, the membership of the Royal St George was growing so rapidly that the club asked the Harbour Commissioners for permission to extend the clubhouse. The second phase was designed by George Papworth, who doubled the size of Mulvany's original building, adding a new western portico and north-facing, apse-ended wing; after 1845 he also added the six-column screen to the south front, and steps from terrace to ground floor on the north front. Papworth was an English-born architect who worked extensively in Ireland, also designing Middleton Park House and Dublin's Pro-Cathedral.

In 1963, the clubhouse and foreshore were renovated and modernised, and in 2008 an addition, the sailing wing, was added to the original clubhouse. The clubhouse and dock are now extensive in size, and mark, in part, the rise of sailing as a leisure pursuit while commercial traffic in the harbour has declined. While sailing and yachting exist as cutting-edge sports driven by new technology, the anchor building of the Royal St George, its clubhouse, speaks to Victorian splendour and the socially privileged nature of the club's origins.

Major redevelopment of the clubhouse and foreshore has taken place since the 1960s and now includes a fully equipped dock, larger and updated facilities and, in 2008, the addition of the new sailing wing, pictured here on the left of the original clubhouse (photo: Royal St George Yacht Club).

THE GORDON BENNETT MOTOR RACE, CARLOW, KILDARE, LAOIS

Several tent villages were established around the course for the use of spectators. The largest, at Ardscull, was organised by the *Motor News* and catered for upwards of 700 people the night before the race (photo: Laois County Library).

The Gordon Bennett Motor Race was the world's first closed-circuit motor race and was held in counties Kildare, Carlow and Laois in 1903. It was the precursor of the Grand Prix and was a huge undertaking for a country which, up until this point, had only about 300 motorcars on its roads. The route of the historic race is now part of Ireland's heritage trail and each year vintage car enthusiasts gather to retrace it. Sport has often been a means of bringing modern ideas and technology to new audiences. Nowhere was this more apparent than in the arrival of an international motor race to Ireland in 1903.

The race was supervised by 2,300 policemen at a cost of over £3,000. Every county in Ireland had to supply a quota based on their resources. Traffic from Dublin to Naas was heavily controlled and all livestock was banished from the roads in the area. It was recorded that 380 cars

In late May 1903 six fatalities in the Paris-to-Madrid motor race led to the fear that all racing would be stopped. This photograph shows Baron Pierre de Caters, who was a Belgian adventurer and aviator as well as a racing driver. He did not finish the Gordon Bennett in 1903 but he did hold the world land speed record the following year (photo: Laois County Library).

were shipped across on the Holyhead–Dublin ferry alone and there were fears that supplies of petrol would run low. Cars from England, France, Germany and America participated in the Gordon Bennett Race, which was to be the central event of two weeks of racing contests across Ireland. Some 1,500 motorists arrived to tour the countryside. Just weeks before the race the districts of Naas and Newbridge were connected telephonically to Dublin. Subscribers were given a list of the numbers and names of those 'on the telephone' in the various towns.

James Gordon Bennett was the proprietor of the *New York Herald* and had funded, among other things, the expedition of Stanley into Africa in search of Dr Livingstone. Bennett sponsored international trophies for balloon and airplane races and, in 1899, he instituted an international racing cup which bore his name. The Gordon Bennett Race had been held in France on previous occasions but a British win in 1902 gave the Automobile Club of Great Britain and Ireland the opportunity to host the event in the following year and it was felt that Ireland, with its smaller population, would be a more practical location.

Those who lobbied to bring the race to Ireland emphasised its economic benefits in terms of spectators and tourists. Moreover, they explained that the race in France had educated the population 'as to the enormous commercial future which lies before the automobile'. It was also hoped that the presence of motoring tourists in Ireland would have the effect of bringing Ireland's roads up to the standards of those in England.

The race was planned for early July 1903. The starting point was Kilrush, near Athy, and the course included two different circuits: a shorter eastern circuit via Kilcullen, Castledermot, Carlow and back to Athy; and a longer western circuit via Kilcullen, Kildare, Monasterevan, Portlaoise, Stradbally and back to Athy. The total distance was 327½ miles.

The cars were dispatched at intervals so that they rarely had to overtake. However, this also made it difficult for spectators to judge who was winning. A grandstand was erected at Kilrush along a stretch of straight road and it cost a guinea to enter the enclosure and a further guinea to mount the stand. Special trains were run from Dublin for the occasion as thousands gathered to watch Camille Jenatzy of Germany, driving a Mercedes, win the race in 6 hours and 39 minutes at an average speed of 49.2 mph. Jenatzy died in a hunting accident in 1913.

The Gordon Bennett Motor Race is now part of the heritage trail and its route is clearly marked through Counties Carlow, Laois and Kildare (photo: Damien Murphy).

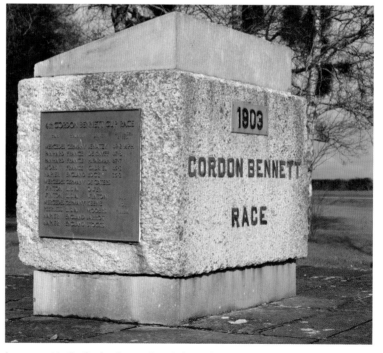

A monument to the Gordon Bennett Race is located at the Moat of Ardscull (stage 16 of the race), at Athy in County Kildare (photo: Damien Murphy).

PEMBROKE HOCKEY CLUB, DUBLIN

Pembroke Wanderers Hockey Club was founded, in the midst of the Irish Civil War, in 1922. The club's location, in Sandymount, Dublin, was a result of the Earl of Pembroke agreeing to make a section of his land in South Dublin available for the playing of hockey. Compared to many other clubs, Pembroke was a latecomer to the game, with clubs such as Naas (1881), Three Rock Rovers (1893) and Dublin University Hockey Club (1893). The Irish Senior Hockey Cup, which began in 1894, is the oldest cup competition for the sport anywhere in the world, and its first winners were the Dundrum Club. The Senior Cup competition for women began in 1904, and the inaugural title was won by the Merton Club. The speed with which Pembroke became a centre of excellence for Irish hockey and a team to be reckoned with was made clear when it won its first women's title in 1931 and men's title in 1934. In the first decade of the twenty-first century, Pembroke won three men's titles and, while the women have not been successful of late, they took the national title at least once

in every decade from the 1930s through to the 1970s. Such was the size of the membership of the club in the 1930s that its annual dinner dance of 1931 was attended by 400 people at the Metropole Hotel and reported in *The Irish Times*. In an era of global economic depression, the simple fact that the dinner dance was so well attended, the dancing went on so long, and that Miss N. Kelly, the organiser of the dance, looked so well in her 'pretty gown of eau de nil lace, worn with a chenille velvet coatee' speaks volumes about the suburban middle class nature of Pembroke's location and membership at the time.

The club has developed steadily over the decades, beginning life with the most basic pavilion and grass pitches, but moving on, in the years since its foundation, so that it now has a full-size, floodlit, water-based, astroturf pitch, as well as a half-size, sand-dressed, astroturf pitch. The clubhouse contains changing rooms, and a bar and function room, and was remodelled in the 1990s. Despite the fitting of the all-weather pitches in the 1980s, flooding

The Wanderers ground occupied land once owned by the Earl of Pembroke, after whom the club is named. The club has developed over the decades, and is now one of the most modern facilities in Ireland (photo: Damien Murphy).

has been a regular problem in the Sandymount area and in 1986, only a week after the pitches had been resurfaced at a cost of thousands, they were under 5ft of water.

The desirability of the area for residential development was obvious in the Celtic Tiger era, and one of the first major redevelopments of the area, Wellington Lodge on Serpentine Avenue, came on stream in 1985, and looked directly over the hockey club. These apartments, which sold at the time for an average price of £800,000, were marketed specifically for the openness that was afforded by overlooking a sporting space. The pressure in the 1990s and early 2000s for green-field sites in the greater south Dublin area, such as sports grounds, that were desirable to build next to (as happened at Pembroke, and also the

Merrion Cricket Club, which had the St Anne's apartments on Anglesea Road built overlooking their open, green spaces) or else on (as with Dun Laoghaire Golf Club, which agreed to sell to developers in 2002), meant that the vistas of many sporting sites have been dramatically changed. While the hockey players of Pembroke go about their business, they are overlooked by apartment dwellers who perhaps appreciate the open space beneath them, but not necessarily the noise of a game in process.

In sports uniforms befitting the demure nature of the age (when it came to societal opinions of women's participation in sport, decency was all), women play hockey in the 1910s. While hockey has always been popular in Catholic girls schools, it was, perhaps because of the GAA's ban on the game, often erroneously seen as the preserve of middle class Protestants (photo: National Library of Ireland).

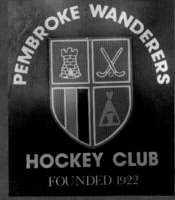

Pembroke Wanderers Hockey Club was founded in 1922, the same year the Free State came into being. Its crest, shown here at the entrance to its Sandymount grounds, depicts the castle of Dublin, the tent of a wanderer, a pair of crossed hockey sticks and the club colours of purple, amber and black (photo: Damien Murphy).

BALLYNAHINCH CASTLE, GALWAY

The waters of the Ballynahinch estate in Connemara were a Mecca for many Irish and non-Irish fishermen. One advantage of the estate was that, while isolated in the wilds of west Galway, it sat on the Galway–Clifden railway line and was served by its own train station (photo: Irish Sporting Heritage).

There has been some form of castle or stronghold at Ballynahinch since the sixteenth century, when it was occupied by the O'Flaherty clan. Famously, Grace O'Malley, the pirate Queen of Connacht, married into the family in the 1540s, and was resident there. The basis of the current house was first constructed by Richard Martin as an inn, and his son, also Richard, was born there. The younger Richard would find fame under the name of Humanity Dick, who as an MP for the area, introduced the Cruelty to Animals Bill in the House of Commons in 1822. In seeking to protect the rights of animals generally the law focused particularly on the working class animal sports of the time such as bear baiting, and cock and dog fighting. It was Martin who was responsible for the ending of pre-modern animal sports and the eventual switch to rational, codified games. Martin was a socialite and well-known dueller who invited many of the notable figures of the period to Ballynahinch, including Daniel O'Connell and Maria Edgeworth, the author of *Castle Rackrent*.

Martin's heirs could not maintain the estate and by the 1850s it had been sold through the Encumbered Estates court and purchased by the London Law Life Assurance Company. It was subsequently sold to Richard Berridge who enlarged the castle to its current size. He also began work on the lakes and rivers around the estate so that they could be used for fishing. In 1924, the Berridges sold the estate to the Maharaja Jam Sahib of Nawangar, more famously known as the record-breaking cricketer Ranji. He spent every summer from 1924 until his death in 1932 at Ballynahinch, and was the owner most responsible for turning the estate into a well-serviced fishing destination. Under Ranji's guidance the gardens were landscaped, and

Fishing was identified early on as a sport that could attract tourists to Ireland. Here, the London, Midland and Scottish Railway use a Norman Wilkinson painting to promote their cross-Irish Sea services in the 1930s (photo: Irish Sporting Heritage).by its own train station (photo: Irish Sporting Heritage).

Above: The successful exploitation of the fishing at Ballynahinch was not simply a matter of developing the hotel and other services, but also in ensuring that the river could be controlled. Here the fisherman's hut sits alongside the old sluice gates that were built to control the flow of the river and ensure that conditions were ideal for the anglers (photo: Irish Sporting Heritage).

Right: In the 1930s, a mass of work was undertaken by the Ballynahinch Estate to ensure optimum fishing conditions. This included the construction of a network of stone-built piers jutting into the river, to allow the most favourable conditions for anglers as they sought their quarry (photo: Irish Sporting Heritage).

Right, inset: The most famous owner of Ballynahinch Castle was Prince Ranjitsinhji, the Maharaja Jam Sahib of Nawangar. A world-famous cricketer, Ranji was introduced to the sports of Ireland by his cricketing friend, C.B. Fry, in particular fishing and hunting. He bought Ballynahinch in 1927 and was responsible for many of the alterations made to the grounds of the estate and the fishing waters. He is commemorated at the entrance to the Castle (photo: Irish Sporting Heritage).

HIS HIGHNESS
SHRI SIR
RANJITSINHJI
VIBHAJI
MAHARAJAH JAM SAHEB OF
NAWANGAR
G.C.S.I. G.B.E. K.C.I.E.
"RANJI"
1872 – 1933
PRINCE OF CRICKETERS
BALLYNAHINCH CASTLE
1927 – 1933

along the river the necessary stone piers and fishing huts were built, as well as sluice gates to control the water's flow, to optimise the fishing conditions. During Ranji's time, the cream of Irish and British society would travel to Ballynahinch to fish, and most would get there by travelling on the Galway-to-Clifden line which included a station at Ballynahinch.

After Ranji's death, the castle had one further private owner before it passed into the hands of the Irish Tourist Board, who opened it as a hotel and fishing venue for the public. It is now run by a corporation, and is seen by many anglers around the world as one of the most desirable places to go fishing. Famed for its fly fishing for salmon and sea trout in the beautiful wilds of Connemara, the annual season runs from February until September, and attracts anglers from around the world. The settled history of Ballynahinch Castle stretches back centuries, and the combination of the historical buildings, a top-rated heritage hotel and some of the finest fly fishing available in Ireland means that it is an important sporting site that continues to attract sportsmen. Its development, particularly by Ranji in the 1920s and 1930s to make best use of the river as a fishery, meant that a wild landscape was effectively tamed for sport. Equally, the transition from private home to hotel and (until 1936) the availability of a rail connection has meant that many visitors have combined their fishing with self-indulgent comfort. Ballynahinch, like many fishing estates in Ireland, is the product of the draw of the landscape, the building of suitable accommodation and the harnessing of the water flows and fish stocks, so that the fame of such angling sites is known across Ireland and beyond.

DONORE HARRIERS, DUBLIN

Donore Harriers was founded in 1893 on Dublin's South Circular Road. Through its early life the club was based in the premises of numerous pubs in the Dolphin's Barn and Kilmainham areas. It was typical of many running clubs across the country in that it survived without a proper clubhouse or facilities. In 1948 Donore Harriers moved into its own premises: a small cottage in Hospital Lane, Islandbridge. This was its home for the next forty-two years.

Donore Harriers had its first success in 1896 in a junior inter-club cross-country race. In this year Dublin jeweller Samuel Waterhouse presented the club with a silver shield for a 10-mile handicap cross-country race. This race, now known as the Waterhouse–Byrne –Baird Shield, has been competed for every year (except 1916) on St Stephen's Day. It is the oldest continuously run club cross-country event in the world.

Organised athletics first came to Ireland in 1857 when foot races were held in Trinity's College Park. Interest in athletics spread throughout the country in the 1870s and the Irish Champion Athletics Club (ICAC) was formed in 1873. Michael Cusack joined the ICAC Council in 1877 but resigned, citing a series of abuses within the organisation, and eventually founded the GAA in 1884. The Irish Amateur Athletics Association (IAAA) was founded in the following year in response to the formation of the GAA and this was the first of a series of rival organisations involved in Irish athletics; the partition of Ireland created further fault lines. Ireland had been represented as a separate entity from Britain in the 1924 Olympics in Paris, but subsequent disputes meant that Ireland was not represented at the 1936 Olympics in Berlin. The repercussions of these disputes within Irish

Like many clubs throughout Ireland Donore Harriers survived for decades without permanent premises. The club was founded in 1893 on the South Circular Road. Following that it was based in the premises of numerous pubs in the Dolphin's Barn and Kilmainham areas (photo: Damien Murphy).

athletics had a very damaging impact on its development and on the provision of facilities for clubs.

Despite this, running clubs have worked hard to provide a sturdy basis for Irish athletics. During the Second World War, Donore Harriers and Clonliffe Harriers held a number of sports meetings that attracted a large attendance due to the fact that many British and some American athletes were stationed in Northern Ireland. To come to a sports meeting in Dublin with good prizes and little shortage of food was a very attractive prospect. In fact, Clonliffe Harriers sports meetings were the premier sports meetings of the athletics season. Guinness sports meetings held in the Iveagh Grounds in Dublin were also attractive but, without foreign athletes taking part, did not have the glamour of the Clonliffe Harriers, Donore Harriers or Civil Services sports meetings.

Money was always tight and Donore's Jimmy Reardon, who competed in the 1948 Olympics in London, found that there was no money to send them to Helsinki in 1952. Reardon was the first foreign athlete to accept a track and field scholarship to the United States. It was not until 1968 that provision was made in the Budget for the spending of £100,000 for sporting bodies in the Republic of Ireland. The international successes of Eamonn Coughlan and

John Treacy in the 1970s and 1980s greatly enhanced the profile of athletics across the country. Twenty thousand people had turned out in Limerick to watch Treacy regain the World Cross Country Championship in 1979.

In 1990 Donore Harriers built a new modern clubhouse on its present location by the banks of the River Liffey. This was augmented in autumn 2007 by the construction of a 300m all-weather rubber-based training track, and field event facilities, located beside the clubhouse. The development of a clubhouse and track represented an enormous achievement for Donore Harriers and has allowed the club to become a central part of the local community. It combines its tradition of Olympians such as Willie Dunne, Bertie Messitt, Tom O'Riordan, Jim McNamara and Basil Clifford with a commitment to the provision of facilities for enthusiastic if less-gifted amateurs.

The introduction of a ladies' section in 1982 has added an important dimension to the club and has reflected the significance of the contribution of women to Irish athletics on the international stage. Donore Harriers, like many other athletics clubs, has worked hard to create and maintain facilities that offer provision for all parts of society, and to value fitness as well as competition

In 1990 a new clubhouse was built on the club's premises at the side of the Liffey. In 2007, a new state-of-the-art track and additional facilities for field events were added (photo: Damien Murphy).

The clubhouse acts as a meeting place and as a reminder of the significant events in the club's history and in the history of Irish athletics (photo: Damien Murphy).

THE RÁS TAILTEANN

The Rás is a very Irish cycling contest. It is rooted in Ireland's landscape, in its politics and history. Initiated in 1953, and formally known as Rás Tailteann, the organisers sought to link the race to Ireland's ancient Tailteann Games, as well as to the contemporary contests held between 1924 and 1932, which were organised as a display of Irish independence and national identity.

The Rás grew out of opposition to partition. Ireland's cycling body, the National Cycling Association (NCA,) had been banned from international competition in 1947 because it refused to accept that it should not have jurisdiction over the six counties in Northern Ireland. Alternative cycling bodies were set up in the Republic and in the North which further undermined the position of the

The first Rás, held in 1953, was a two-day event that wore its politics on its sleeve. The second day of racing was preceded by a ceremony and wreath-laying at the monument in Wexford commemorating the 1798 Rebellion of the United Irishmen. The photograph shows Pat Murphy and the Lord Mayor of Wexford (photo: originally published in *The Rás: The Story of Ireland's Unique Bike Race* by Tom Daly).

When it was decided to extend the Rás to eight days in 1954, there were widespread misgivings about the ability of NCA riders to race 1,000 miles in that time. The Rás has always been a gruelling physical test and this photograph evokes the sense of commitment and determination it takes to complete the race (photo: originally published in *The Rás: The Story of Ireland's Unique Bike Race* by Tom Daly).

Right: The 1954 programme shows the very deliberate all-island nature of the Rás, from Ballymena in the north to Bantry in the south (photo: originally published in *The Rás: The Story of Ireland's Unique Bike Race* by Tom Daly).

NCA. It was therefore deemed necessary to organise a national race of sufficient stature to rival international competitions. The first race, a two-day event, began at the GPO in Dublin after a wreath-laying ceremony at the statue of Cúchulainn. The second stage was preceded by a ceremony at the 1798 monument in Wexford and it was clear that the Rás was in large part an expression of Irish republican politics.

The Rás is not part of Ireland's built heritage yet it was an event that used the physical landscape of monuments and geography to make political points. Controversy was occasionally courted when the race (and the Irish tricolour) crossed the border into Northern Ireland. From the 1960s the Rás programme was also used by Joe Christle (one of the race's founders and its driving force) as a vehicle for political messages. Christle provided articles which expounded on everything from Irish history to apartheid in South Africa. Each year he dedicated the Rás to such diverse figures as Roger Casement, St Patrick, the Irish Christian Brothers and the Fenians. The fact that early winners of the Rás were cyclists who effectively excluded themselves from international racing on a point of principal also locates the origins of the race in a very specific period of Irish history, when the anti-partition movement was very strong.

The second Rás, in 1954, was an eight-day event that set the standard for the future and is seen as a watershed in Irish cycle racing. It was a great success, despite the difficulty of obtaining sponsorship. The circuit of just under 1,000 miles was routed through the Irish countryside, providing great spectacles and social

Bord Fáilte recognised the potential of the Rás as a showcase for the Irish landscape. The Rás is the longest-running sponsored event in Irish sport. Cyclists are seen here entering the Kerry Mountains heading for Moll's Gap in 1955 (photo: originally published in *The Rás: The Story of Ireland's Unique Bike Race* by Tom Daly).

The Rás passing homes by the side of the road in the 1950s (photo: originally published in *The Rás: The Story of Ireland's Unique Bike Race* by Tom Daly).

occasions. The existing networks of the GAA, the NCA and the National Cycling and Athletic Association, as well as that of local republicans, were mobilised across the country to help with organisation, and local cycling clubs and county teams competed.

As members of the NCA were denied the right to compete in international competition they organised a protest at the 1956 World Championships in Frascati to highlight the political position of the Association, and gained widespread publicity as well as a spell in an Italian jail. Protests at the 1972 Munich Olympics took place in a very different international climate and were received with little tolerance. The deteriorating political situation in Northern Ireland also eventually led to the development of co-operation between all the cycling bodies in Ireland, under a tripartite committee, in 1978. The first commercial sponsorship deal was brokered in 1974 with Bord Fáilte, and the 'Discover Ireland Rás Tailteann' was seen as a perfect showcase for the Irish countryside as a holiday destination.

In succeeding decades the Rás developed into an increasingly professional event and gained a 2.5 ranking from the Union Cycliste Internationale in 2001, which made it a points race for the Olympic Games and World Cycling Championships. It now attracts the world's top cyclists.

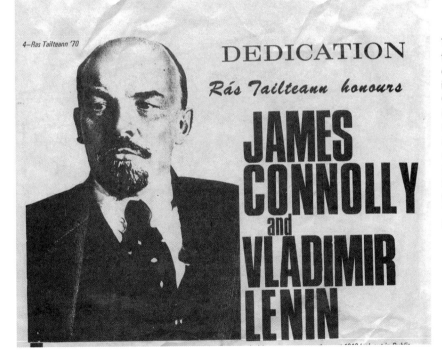

4–Ras Tailteann '70

DEDICATION

Rás Tailteann honours

JAMES CONNOLLY and VLADIMIR LENIN

Teams from behind the Iron Curtain defied the Union Cycliste Internationale directive on the NCA and a Polish team competed in 1963, while a team from Czechoslovakia came in 1968. An invitation to the Russian team was the most ambitious and included the assurance that the 1970 Rás would be dedicated to Lenin. A mixture of vodka, diplomacy and the promise of room and board obtained the Russians' agreement to attend (photo: originally published in *The Rás: The Story of Ireland's Unique Bike Race* by Tom Daly).

In 1987 Stephen Roche was the only rider to emulate Eddie Merckx's feat of a victory in the Tour de France, Giro d'Italia and World Championship in one year. When Merckx first met Roche after his triple win, he congratulated him, saying: 'Congratulations, Stephen, we are equal now.' Roche quipped: 'No, we're not, Eddie: you've never won the Rás.' Roche is seen here in 1979, in the year he won the Rás aged nineteen (photo: originally published in *The Rás: The Story of Ireland's Unique Bike Race* by Tom Daly).

THE NORTH WEST 200, ANTRIM AND DERRY

The North West 200 is the biggest sporting event in Ireland and has become the most popular road racing event for motorbikes in the world. Each year between 100,000 and 150,000 people gather along the north coast around the triangle circuit of Coleraine, Portrush and Portstewart to watch international racers negotiate 8.9 miles of public roads. The event is heavily reliant on the work of volunteers who lay out over 4,000 safety bales and erect several miles of protective fencing in order to prepare the temporary course.

Motor racing in Ireland enjoyed a significant degree of success in the early twentieth century. The Motor Cycle Union of Ireland (MCUI) was founded in 1902 by a group of men who came mainly from the motorcycle and cycle trades. Among their number was John C. Cooney who had won the very first motor race to be held in Ireland, at Navan Cycling and Athletic Grounds on August 15 1900, riding an Ariel tricycle. In the first decades of the century legal and illegal races were held on public roads across the country.

The Motor Vehicles Races Act (NI) was one of the earliest pieces of legislation passed by the new Northern Ireland Government in May 1922. It permitted County Councils to close public roads for the purpose of allowing car and motorcycle racing to take place. The new administration saw motor racing as a way to promote car manufacturing in Northern Ireland and to attract British tourists, and it heavily promoted the sport. The first major road racing event to be held in Ireland was the 1922 Ulster Grand Prix. It took place on the 20.5 mile Clady circuit in County Antrim and was considered a resounding success. The Leinster 100 was the first road race to be held

in the Free State. It took place in 1923 at a circuit at Dunshaughlin, County Meath, and was run under a special permit from the authorities.

The first North West 200, organised by the City of Derry Motorcycle Club, was held on 20 April 1929. The decision to hold the race over 200 miles firmly established it as a rigorous test that factory teams could not ignore. The first meeting provided quite a spectacle. The Union flag and the Irish tricolour – in honour of the six competitors from the Free State – flew above the large crowd. A grandstand was erected along with a marquee where refreshments were sold. A brass band entertained spectators.

Although some racing took place during the Second World War petrol shortages meant that motorcycle racing was almost at a complete stop by 1941 and the North West 200 was suspended until 1947. The Motor Cycle Union of Ireland responded to the changing circumstances by organising some bicycle trials to keep interest alive.

In 1959 the North West 200 became a 200-mile event in name only and the new race programme provided four separate races run over shorter distances. Coleraine and District Motor Club took over the running of the event in 1964 (from the North of Ireland Motor Club) and inherited an event in the doldrums. The security issues of the 1970s brought further problems, and pressure from the authorities led to the cancellation of the 1972 meeting as large public gatherings were considered to be potential flashpoints.

By the end of the twentieth century the North West 200 had re-established itself as a premier event in the motor sport calendar. Road racing has continued to be the

A speed trial on Magilligan Strand in 1923. Races took place on beaches in the years before Road Closing Orders. Both Ulster and Irish Championship races took place at Magilligan and racing continued here, in some degree, until the 1930s. Sand racing also took place near Dublin and on other suitable beaches. The first fatality in Irish motorcycle sport took place at Portmarnock Strand, Dublin, in 1913 (photo: Morton Archive).

most popular branch of motorcycle racing. However, it has faced many questions over safety and, having been widespread across Europe, is now primarily associated with the Isle of Man and Ireland. The North West 200 is heavily reliant on sponsorship as the event is free to spectators. It is an event that combines the professionalism and finance of international event organisers and sponsors with the voluntary commitment of local people who often take their annual holiday to coincide with the event.

Above: Motor racing was heavily promoted by the new Northern Irish government and the Motor Vehicles Races Act (NI) was one of the earliest pieces of legislation it passed, in May 1922 (programme and information: Ballymoney Museum).

Right: After the Second World War, fuel rationing prevented a full programme of Ulster road racing taking place. Special permission was granted by the Ministry of Fuel and Power and petrol was allocated for the North West 200 in 1947 and 1949 (programme and information: Ballymoney Museum).

Left: A memorial garden to Joey Dunlop was opened in May 2001. The bronze statue was created by Amanda Barton. Joey Dunlop was the most successful motorcycle road racer of all time. Among his celebrated achievements were twenty-six wins at the Isle of Man TT, twenty-four wins at the Ulster Grand Prix, thirteen wins at the North West 200 and five TT Formula One World Motorcycle Championships. Joey Dunlop died in 2000 while racing in Estonia. The memorial garden was sponsored by Honda (photo: Ballymoney Museum).

11
SITE-SPECIFIC HERITAGE

BIG HOUSE: AVONDALE, WICKLOW

Built in 1777, Avondale played host to all sports from cricket and croquet to Gaelic games (photo: Irish Sporting Heritage).

Charles Stewart Parnell's father, John Henry, is credited with introducing cricket to Wicklow, and founded the county club around 1835. John Henry was a leading member of the Phoenix Club, Ireland's oldest cricket club. This photograph shows the area on which he laid out an impressive cricket ground at Avondale. It was the main cricket ground in Wicklow until the 1860s (photo: Irish Sporting Heritage).

Charles Stewart Parnell's grandfather acquired Aghavannagh Barracks on the Military Road in Wicklow in 1825 and the family used it as a hunting lodge. John Redmond bought the barracks after Parnell's death in 1891, and it later came into use as a youth hostel, being finally put out of commission in 1998 (photo: Irish Sporting Heritage).

Wicklow County Cricket Club (the result of a merger of Avondale and North Wicklow cricket clubs in 2009) still plays some matches at Rathdrum Rugby Club, maintaining the tradition of cricket within the vicinity of Avondale (photo: Irish Sporting Heritage).

Ireland's big houses were crucibles for the development of sport. The landed elite organised tennis tournaments and played croquet, cricket and archery matches when they gathered for social occasions. Landowners also provided the sites on which sporting clubs could be established and it was under their patronage that many sports flourished across their demesne.

The seat of the Parnell family at Avondale, County Wicklow, was built in 1777 by James Wyatt, a London architect with a thriving country house practice in Ireland. The Georgian house was built on 3,807 acres and had a rent roll of £1,789 when Charles Stewart Parnell inherited it on coming of age in 1867. In its sporting heritage Avondale is interesting both for its place within the social life of the surrounding countryside and because, as the home of one of Ireland's most significant politicians, it brought together a range of sporting worlds.

Charles Stewart Parnell fished, shot, hunted, rode, played billiards, cricket and hockey. He participated in all the sports traditionally associated with Ireland's big houses. His father, John Henry, is credited with introducing cricket to Wicklow, and founded the county club around 1835. John Henry Parnell was a leading member of the Phoenix Club, Ireland's oldest cricket club, and laid out an impressive cricket ground at Avondale. In common with other members of the landed gentry he received his education in England. It was at Eton and at Cambridge University that he developed a knowledge of English sports and was keen to promote them on his return to Ireland. This movement of wealthy young men between the two countries was a crucial element in the diffusion of sports across Ireland. Charles Stewart Parnell was introduced to cricket in his nursery days and continued his interest throughout his life. He was, however, no more than an average player and never attended matches after he entered Parliament.

Sporting gatherings in country houses were confined to a limited social group of the landowning class and their social equals, primarily members of the military. Parnell's twenty-first birthday was marked by a three-day cricket match between officers of the Dublin garrison and the Wicklow county side. A military band, tents, marquees and speeches added to the festivities.

In the winter foxhunting was the most popular sport among the gentry and it also provided a focus for hospitality and entertainment. Parnell's grandfather had acquired Aghavannagh Barrack on the Military Road in Wicklow in 1825 and the family used it as a hunting lodge. John Henry Parnell was Master of the Hounds and kept a pack at Avondale. However, he did not hunt after his eldest son Hayes died from a hunting accident aged sixteen. Charles Stewart Parnell was also a member of the hunting fraternity and subscribed to the Wicklow harriers. He therefore avoided supporting those Land Leaguers who used anti-hunt agitation to protest against the government's treatment of League leaders in the 1880s.

In 1884, Parnell accepted the invitation to become a patron of the newly established GAA and thereafter Avondale played host to Gaelic games. In 1886 a tournament of six football matches attracted an attendance of 12,000 who arrived on special excursion trains laid on from Wexford to Rathdrum and from Dublin. Several Wicklow championship games were also played at Avondale in 1887. The GAA remained loyal to Parnell after the scandal of his involvement with the O'Shea divorce case, and was almost ruined as an organisation as a result. At his death it was decided that every member of the GAA attending his funeral would carry a hurley, supplied by the Dublin Committee. As the funeral cortège moved from the City Hall towards Glasnevin cemetery the members of parliament present marched on each side of the hearse and acted as pallbearers. Immediately behind came at least 2,000 members of the GAA 'bearing their camans on each of which was a knot of crepe and a green ribbon'.

PRIVATE SCHOOL:
WILSON'S HOSPITAL, WESTMEATH

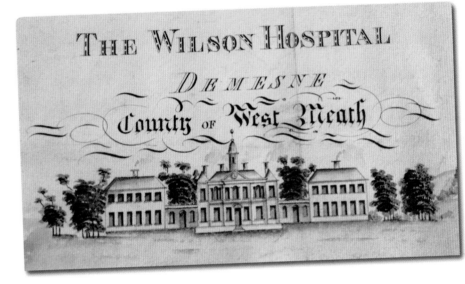

Opened in 1761, Wilson's Hospital was designed by John Pentland, and built in the Palladian style (photo: Wilson's Hospital).

Wilson's Hospital School, near Multyfarnham, County Westmeath, opened its doors in 1761, to its first student, Arthur Hill. The school came into being as a result of the will of Andrew Wilson, who envisaged a school alongside a hospital for elderly Protestant men. The design for the main building was attributed to John Portland. The school was the site of a battle between government forces and the United Irishmen in September 1798, and over 150 insurgents were killed there, in what became known as the Battle of Wilson's Hospital. By the 1830s, the school had grown so that its pupil roll totalled 160 boys, there to be given a Protestant education and in 1969, after the Preston School in Navan closed, it became, as it remains, a co-educational boarding and day school. The school was served by Multyfarnham railway station, which lay not far

from the school gates, from 1855 until 1963, and which was part of the Mullingar-to-Sligo line.

It is clear from the layout of fields around the school, known as 'The Forty Acres', that sport probably entered the consciousness of the boys at the school in the nineteenth century, and it is likely that cricket was the first codified game to be played there. The forty acres now encompass playing surfaces for cricket, rugby, hockey and soccer, with rugby having arrived at the school in the late 1830s and the first captain of a school rugby team being recorded in 1840. Despite being one of the oldest rugby-playing schools in Ireland, it took until 1934 before the rugby team made its first appearance in the Leinster Schools Junior Cup. In rugby, as with many other sports, the school has, in addition to entering national and

Built in 1761, the John Pentland-designed Wilson's Hospital celebrated its 250th anniversary in 2011 and continues to welcome new generations of pupils through its doors (photo: Alison Burns).

provincial competitions, also played a regular series of fixtures against other local and Protestant schools. It has been particularly successful in girls' hockey and cricket. Wilson's is fascinating in that it is, by comparison with other schools, relatively small, and has a long history of co-education when many other schools choose to remain single sex. The intimacy of the school's sporting architecture, given its small size, is obvious in the layout of the grounds. The eighteenth-century main school building is not set apart from the business of sport, but rather the sports grounds were laid out directly behind the school which, in the absence of changing rooms and showers, would have allowed students to return indoors as soon the game was complete. Even today, the main sporting structure from an earlier time, the cricket pavilion, stands within a few feet of the rear of the school buildings.

Despite being a small school, Wilson's, in line with most private schools in Ireland, has developed its sporting infrastructure. Grass pitches have been replaced where necessary with all-weather pitches, and floodlights have been constructed to allow the playing day to be lengthened. An outdoor swimming pool was added (but remains unused for much of the year, given the weather), and in 2001 the construction of an indoor sports hall was completed. In heritage terms, Wilson's, as with the few other schools in the country with eighteenth-century origins, is important for its original buildings. It was built in a Palladian style to designs by John Pentland between 1759 and 1761, and in the view of the National Inventory of Architectural Heritage, represents one of the finest and most sophisticated mid-Georgian buildings constructed outside of Dublin. Its few sporting structures are of little architectural value in themselves, but the school is a prime example of sporting heritage given the longevity of sporting activity on the forty acres, which are still in use today.

'The Forty Acres' was not only the place where the boys (and later the girls) of Wilson's Hospital played, but it was also where they were made to watch. School spirit was not simply formed on the field of play at such schools, but also through the communal support of the team. Here, boys watch a rugby game in the 1950s (photo: Wilson's Hospital).

The cricket pavilion is one of the older sporting buildings remaining at the school. The majority of older structures have been demolished and replaced by state-of-the-art buildings in recent years (photo: Irish Sporting Heritage).

The outdoor swimming pool was a common sight at many Irish schools, and Wilson's was no exception. The problems with outdoor pools are the costs of maintenance, their unsuitability for use across many months of the year, and the dangers posed by open water in a school setting. The pool is now enclosed, and the grey building behind it on the left is the new indoor sports hall (photo: Irish Sporting Heritage).

UNIVERSITY: TRINITY COLLEGE DUBLIN

Trinity College has been one of the most significant centres of sport in Ireland. Founded in 1592, it educated the country's protestant elite and therefore played an important role in the diffusion of sports across the country. Trinity-educated men promoted various games both through patronage and by example. The College, which was originally located outside the city walls, initially banned games being played within its confines; however, a bowling green and five courts were laid out at the end of the seventeenth century and a real tennis court in 1741. None of these has survived. It was in the middle of the nineteenth century, with the modernisation of sporting practices, that Trinity established itself as a focus for a variety of newly formed clubs, and pitches were laid out

The first modern athletics meeting in Ireland was held in Trinity's College Park in 1857 (photo: National Library of Ireland).

for cricket (1842) and football (1854). Indeed, the Football Club at Trinity is the oldest rugby club in continuous existence. The number of men attending Trinity who had received an education in England increased significantly in the mid-nineteenth century and this had implications for the spread of codified games throughout Ireland.

The first modern athletics meeting to be held in Ireland was in College Park in 1857. Organised by the Football Club, and entitled 'Dublin University Football Club Foot Races', it was attended by the Lord Lieutenant along with a large and enthusiastic crowd. Such was its popularity that it was restaged a month later and eventually the Foot Races Committee evolved into the University Athletic Club in 1872. For a quarter of a century the College Races were considered the greatest fashionable outdoor event of the year in Dublin. However, in 1880 the College imposed restrictions on the races in order to curb their more unruly excesses and they gradually fell out of fashion. Their financial success, however, provided the income for the building of a pavilion on College Park in 1884. It

Above: Trinity Pavilion was built in 1884 and was designed by Thomas Drew (photo: National Library of Ireland).

Below: Trinity Pavilion continues to be a central part of college life (photo: Damien Murphy).

Trinity College initially banned games being played within its confines; however, sport became an increasingly important part of university life (photo: Damien Murphy).

continues to be an important visual, social and sporting site within the college. The architect Thomas Drew designed a building in the Roman Doric style and it was completed at a cost of £1,500.

Political developments had an impact on sporting life in Trinity. Sheep grazed on College Park during the First World War as athletics ceased, and the Officers' Training Corps commandeered the gymnasium. The cricket ground became a meadow during these years and the tennis courts (constructed in 1879) ceased to exist. During the War of Independence a female undergraduate was killed while watching a cricket match between the Gentlemen of Ireland and the Military in College Park when a gunman opened fire through the railings (along Nassau Street).

Membership of Trinity sports clubs had, at times, unforeseen benefits. The Swimming Club, founded in 1897, had among its members the redoubtable Oliver St John Gogarty who, as a 45-year-old Free State Senator was kidnapped by Republicans during the Civil War and escaped by swimming the Liffey. He later presented the river, in thanksgiving, with two swans.

The sporting tradition continues at Trinity and fifty sports clubs are affiliated to the Dublin University Central Athletic Club. The college opened a new Sports Centre in 2008. Its swimming pool, sports halls and climbing frame indicate the way in which sporting activities have been moved indoors in the twenty-first century.

Fifty sports clubs are affiliated to the Dublin University Central Athletic Club (photo: Trinity College Dublin).

In 2008 Trinity opened a new sports centre, which comprises a 25-metre, 6-lane swimming pool with a movable floor and two sports halls, as well as a climbing wall, which is visible for almost the entire height of the building from Westland Row (photo: Trinity College Dublin).

WORKPLACE: ALSAA, DUBLIN

The tradition of a work-based sporting club is one that has its roots in nineteenth-century philanthropy and the extensive provision of sporting amenities for the workers of Guinness would be a classic example from that period. In 1936, Ireland's newest state company came into being, namely Aer Lingus. In its first few years the company was small, and operated from the Baldonnell aerodrome, before moving to Dublin airport in 1940. With the ending of the Second World War and the expansion of the airline's routes, staff numbers grew rapidly in the late 1940s, and the employees of the airline began to organise themselves socially. Through the pages of the staff newsletter, *Aer Sceala*, the various sporting and leisure pursuits organised by employees were heavily promoted. The increased sporting activity of the airline staff quickly led to the formation of an umbrella organisation in 1948: the Aer Lingus Social and Athletic Association (ALSAA).

The first premises for the club were at Beresford Place in the city centre. Here the staff would gather for social evenings and meetings of each of the different athletics branches. Although Beresford Place served as ALSAA clubhouse it had, beyond a dart board and snooker table, no sporting facilities of its own. The various sporting groups within ALSAA rented pitches and courts across the city so that they could play their games. To rectify this situation, ALSAA moved in 1965 to rented sporting premises at Foster Avenue, Stillorgan. While there were the clubhouse and the pitches necessary for some games, the site was not big enough for the 6,000 Aer Lingus employees (and their families) of the time.

In 1971, ALSAA made the obvious move and relocated to the airport. The first premises included a bar, offices and sporting facilities for snooker, tennis, soccer, rugby, darts

When ALSAA first began life at Beresford Place, the sporting opportunities in-house were limited. Sports, such as they were, usually revolved around the dart and chess boards (photo: Aer Lingus).

and squash. The expansion of ALSAA facilities at the airport continued that year with the opening of a purpose-built swimming pool, which had a small gymnasium attached. While the airport facilities were a great improvement on anything ALSAA had occupied in the past, the buildings and pitches were, with the exception of the swimming pool, adaptations of existing spaces, and not purpose built. With the expansion of Aer Lingus and the airport's activities in the 1980s, the decision was made that ALSAA would have to leave its facility (which is where hangar six now stands). This time, with the assistance of the airline and the airport, a purpose-built facility, standing on some 72 acres of land, was constructed. The Aer Rianta architect Declan O'Dwyer was given the brief to design the new facility, and in 1982 it opened its doors. The building takes its architectural lead not from the dominant design ideas of the early 1980s but rather is inspired by the modernism of Desmond FitzGerald's original terminal at Dublin airport. The sleek, clean lines of the ALSAA building, with its curved glass and white walls, would make most passers-by believe that the building had been standing since the 1930s rather than the 1980s.

ALSAA's operations now extend to supporting thirty sporting and social clubs, while they regularly make their facilities available to the wider north Dublin community near the airport. In doing so they also support Tag Rugby, GAA, Taekwon-do and soccer teams from the local area. At the start of the twenty-first century, the very idea of workplace philanthropy had shifted from its nineteenth-century origins to include sportsmen and women from beyond the company. Also, the industrial unit of the large state, or semi-state body, to which employees were fiercely loyal and imagined working in their whole lives, was something that largely died away from the 1980s. That ALSAA still exists, close to the daily place of work for the airport's employees, is a sign of the enthusiasm that its members bring to it, and the enjoyment they take from their workplace sport.

The current ALSAA building near Dublin airport is one of the most complete sports venues in the city. Still hugely popular with airport staff, the venue is also open to other local clubs (photo: Aer Lingus).

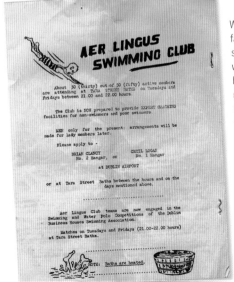

Without its own facilities, the sportsmen and women of ALSAA had to borrow or rent sporting venues. Here, in the early 1950s, the swimming club announces its weekly gathering at the Tara Street Baths (photo: Aer Lingus).

PRIVATE: WOODBROOK GOLF CLUB, WICKLOW

It is clear from the history of sport that many sporting sites begin life as the private indulgence of wealthy individuals. One such individual, who was a keen pleasure seeker, was Sir Stanley Herbert Cochrane. He was the heir to, and later governing director and chairman of, the Cantrell & Cochrane mineral water business. He had a city home on Kildare Street in Dublin, but enjoyed the spaces of his seaside home, Corke Lodge, Woodbrook, just outside Bray.

It was at Woodbrook where Cochrane indulged his whims. In 1907 he established the Woodbrook Cricket Club, and built one of the finest grounds of the period, which included a large pavilion, just behind his house. Such were his connections and the beauty of the club's setting that he was able to bring a touring Australian test team to Ireland to play at Woodbrook. *The Irish Times* recorded how 'the charming ground looked its best, and the visitors were loud in its praise, as was only natural, considering the beauty of its surroundings and the magnificent wicket that had been prepared'. Despite the enthusiasm for his pitch and clubhouse, Cochrane's enjoyment of cricket lasted only five years, when he closed the club and turned his attention to music and built a concert hall in his grounds. This attracted some of the major acts of the pre-First World War era including John McCormack and Nellie Melba, as well as the London Symphony and Hallé Orchestras.

During the First World War, in which he served, Cochrane was created a baronet in 1915, for his patronage of music and sport, as well as his work for prisoners of war. Throughout the War, he used his Kildare Street house as a centre for sending parcels to those who had been captured by the Germans. In 1921, two years before he sold his business and moved to England, Cochrane indulged his last sporting passion in Ireland and laid out a nine-hole golf course at Woodbrook. In 1926, the members of the club were able to take over the management of Woodbrook, and in 1928 they agreed a 21-year lease on the course at a rent of £850 per annum. One of the attractions of Woodbrook for its members was its proximity to the railway. Until 1956, the club had an agreement with the railway company, which allowed members sitting in the bar to press a switch that would cause the next train to stop for two minutes and collect the players on their way home.

After taking control of the club, the members used the old cricket pavilion as their clubhouse, and meals were taken in part of Cochrane's original house. Such a set-up was clearly undesirable, and in the mid-1950s the clubhouse was doubled in size, and a bar, billiards and card room were added. The cricket pavilion remains at the heart of the clubhouse, although now surrounded on both sides by further additions. Woodbrook was one of the best-run private clubs in the post-Second World War period, as evidenced by the staging of the first major professional golf tournament in Ireland at the course, the Hennessey, in 1958. This was followed by the Irish Hospitals Sweepstakes tournament in 1959 and the Carrolls International from 1963. It was attended by the main European and some United States professionals of the time. When talk started about reviving the Irish Open, which had been discontinued in 1953, Woodbrook was the obvious tried-and-tested venue. Christy O'Connor Jnr beat off an international field, including that year's Open champion, Tom Watson, to take the title and £5,000 prize money. To date, Woodbrook has hosted eighteen international tournaments, more than any other Irish course.

Woodbrook Golf Club began life as the private home and sporting dream of Sir Stanley Herbert Cochrane. Before he laid out the first nine-hole course on the site, it was used for cricket. Here, the original cricket pavilion has been built into the golf clubhouse and stands as a reminder of the game that went before. The photographs of the course show how on one side the course is bordered by Dublin Bay, which challenges golfers, and on the other by the DART line, which once allowed players to travel home (photo: Irish Sporting Heritage/Woodbrook Golf Course).

The product of one man's sporting enthusiasm, Woodbrook is a legendary site in the annals of Irish golf. It grew from the visions of one man, and was carefully managed by the club's members and managements to host international golf tournaments at a time when such events were rare in Ireland. One wonders how many of the international golfers of the 1960s and 1970s realised that they were playing on a course that began life as a cricket pitch, or that they were changing in a clubhouse that had been built around the former cricket pavilion

MULTISPORT: PHOENIX PARK, DUBLIN

The area that has become known as the Phoenix Park was part of a land grant made by Strongbow in 1174. In the seventeenth century the government obtained the land and it housed the official residence of the Irish Viceroys. It was during this period that the area was developed as a park. Since then the Phoenix Park has been a celebrated site of sport in Ireland and is one of the largest enclosed recreational spaces within any European capital city.

The histories of cricket and polo in Ireland are closely connected to the Phoenix Park. Cricket was first played in the Fifteen Acres, an old duelling ground, in August 1792, when an eleven of the garrison played an all-Ireland side. The Phoenix Club was not founded until 1830, but it was the first cricket club in the country and is believed to be the third oldest in the world. The club moved to its current ground in 1846 and, despite being damaged by a German bomb in 1941, the site is one of the oldest in unbroken use in the world. The Civil Service Cricket Club, founded in 1863 when the Lord Lieutenant persuaded parliament to give civil servants their own pitch. By 1900 there were twenty cricket grounds in the Phoenix Park but now only two survive.

Nine Acres is the home of the polo ground. Founded in 1873, the All-Ireland Polo Club is the oldest polo club in Ireland and the second oldest in Europe. Its members included the country's privileged classes and polo established itself as a popular and fashionable pastime. The area near the polo grounds made international headlines when the Chief Secretary for Ireland and the Permanent Undersecretary were murdered there in 1882 by a Fenian group known as the Invincibles. Such was the popularity of polo that a new ground was acquired for the County Dublin Polo Club in 1888. Polo cup matches were held at the end of the week of Dublin Horse Show and were part of the general social festivities. The polo ground was also the venue for hurling in the years before the formation of the GAA and for Bohemian FC matches. Bohemians carried goalposts to and from North Circular Road Lodge where they were stored. The Victorian pavilion at the polo ground, like almost all such structures in Ireland, has not survived. It was seriously damaged by fire in January 1987 but has since been restored to a larger version of its original.

As a hub of sporting life for Dublin's military and gentry, the Phoenix Park was an obvious place of interest for visitors to the Horse Show, and in 1902 the opening of a racecourse furthered this appeal. The annual Phoenix Plate for two-year-olds was held until 1913 and was the richest race in the country, surpassing even the Irish Derby at the time. The Phoenix Park Racecourse reached the height of its popularity in the 1950s but by the early 1980s had been sold to a developer and was eventually bought by members of a racing syndicate; however, it failed to attract crowds. Racing was discontinued in October 1990 and arson attacks and neglect have meant that none of the original structures has survived. The Royal Dublin Golf Club was also located in the Phoenix Park for a few years before relocating to Bull Island at Clontarf in 1889.

In the twentieth century the Phoenix Park continued to offer a natural home for a multitude of sporting events. Moments of great spectacle were joined by the daily commitment of amateurs on the many pitches that have been laid out. The Rás Tailteann includes a 50km speed circuit in the Phoenix Park and, in 1998, cyclists competing in the Tour de France visited the Park on 12 July as part of their journey to the finishing line in Paris. The Dublin Marathon also passes through the Phoenix Park.

PÁIRC NA LÚTCLEASAÍOCTA
SPORTS GROUNDS

Above: The Polo Club was founded in 1873. It was the first polo ground established in Ireland and the second in Europe. Here, at the end of the nineteenth century, the annual married versus single men challenge match is depicted (photo: Office of Public Works).

Left: Throughout its history the Phoenix Park has been the home of multiple sports including athletics, cricket, cycling, GAA, golf, horse racing, motor racing, polo, rugby and soccer (photo: Damien Murphy).

In 1929 over 100,000 people gathered to watch the International Motor Race, or Grand Prix, in the Phoenix Park. To create an uninterrupted line, the Phoenix Column was moved to the side of the road, where it remained for many decades. The Free State government provided a grant of £3,000 and races took place again in 1930 and 1931. In 1932 Fianna Fáil removed the subvention for what they saw as a rich man's game. However motor racing continues in the Phoenix Park, though not annually, and Formula 1 stars such as Damon Hill and Jacques Villeneuve have appeared on the circuit.

A series of pitches has been laid out in Fifteen Acres catering primarily for Gaelic games and soccer. The provision, although basic, is nevertheless extensive. The custom was that on payment to the park ranger, teams received use of the pavilion, a pitch and two corner flags. The issuing of the flags made it easy to see who had paid their subs. Dublin Camogie County Board also has its home in Phoenix Park, and has recently erected a new pavilion. The Irish Army and Garda Síochána also continue to have pitches in the Park.

The expanse of the Phoenix Park contains within itself elements of all parts of Irish sporting history. It has moved from being a playground of the privileged classes to a vast space of publically accessible sporting sites and events; a vast area that celebrates the place of sport in Irish life.

James Butler, Duke of Ormond, developed the area as a park in the 1660s and introduced deer, partridge and peasants. Poaching and wandering deer led to the building of a wall around the extensive grounds (photo: Peter Higgins).

Although the original polo pavilion was burnt down in the 1980s, it was rebuilt using the old plans so that it still appears as near to the original as possible (photo: Louise Farrell).

The Phoenix Cricket Club moved to its current site in 1846, vacating its old ground to accommodate the widening of the road through the park. The move was financed by the Board of Works at a cost of £73 (photo: Damien Murphy).

SPORTING MEMORIALS

One of three statues erected to memorialise Master McGrath in Ireland, this one in Dungarvan is the most famous. Originally placed on private land, the memorial was eventually moved to its public spot. The fame of the dog stretched beyond his Waterloo Cup feats and was the subject of a famous Dubliners ballad, Master McGrath (photo: Damien Murphy).

Sporting events and heroes become part of the fabric of national life. Collectively, societies remember and recall the key sporting events of their lifetime. Great finals or matches are brought to mind in home and pub conversations, as are the merits of the best players or those who achieved victories in international events. Occasionally civic authorities, communities, clubs and individuals decide to honour the heroes of yesteryear and their achievements.

In the process of memorialising the sporting events and heroes of Ireland, public spaces around the country have become sites of commemoration. These vary in size and scale, from small memorials associated with a club or parish, to major sculptural commissions erected by town, city or county authorities. The style of the statues differs depending on who, or what, is being memorialised. The most figurative are those honouring former athletes, which depict the sportsperson in action, such as that of Tony Byrne (bronze medal winner in boxing at the 1956 Olympics) in Drogheda or Paddy Ryan (gold medal winner in the hammer, representing the US, in 1920) in Pallas Green, County Limerick. More recently, Drogheda has honoured the sporting lives of the handballer Joey Maher and boxer Tony Byrne, with statues created by the sculptor Laury Dizengremel.

Other styles of statue celebrate the ties between place and sport, such as that which celebrates the links between Kerry and its strong tradition in Gaelic football. The statue in Tralee features players jumping for a ball, but they are generic figures, not named stars from the past. The celebration is of Kerry football and its links to the county rather than any specific players.

Patrick Ryan won his Olympic gold medal as a hammer thrower under the American flag in 1920. He returned to Ireland to run the family farm in 1924, and died in 1964. This statue, in his home village of Pallas Green, County Limerick, celebrates his most famous exploit (photo: Damien Murphy).

As well as people, events have also been memorialised such as the site of the first All-Ireland football final (Donnybrook in Dublin) or the town where the first ever steeplechase was started (Buttevant, County Cork). In addition to formal and informal acts of remembrance and memorialisation depicting events and people in civic and public spaces, the sporting lives of individuals have also been remembered at the time of their burial. Headstones around the country commemorate the sporting lives of those buried there, whether famous star or local amateur player, such as the headstone of the boxer Jack Doyle, in the Cobh graveyard, that features a pair of boxing gloves.

In Ballymoney, County Antrim, a memorial in honour of legendary motorcyclist Joey Dunlop depicts the racer on his motorbike.

While Ireland probably has fewer sporting memorials and statues than many other countries, the acts of constructing and dedicating such civic markers of the sporting past are important in that they celebrate the centrality of sporting legends and events to the locality where they are placed. They acknowledge the importance of sport within the community, and mark those spaces and people that were significant.

Rosmuc, County Galway, is probably most connected, in boxing terms, with Sean Mannion, who fought for a world title in the mid 1980s. However, in the village itself, outside the GAA ground, it is another boxer – Mike Flaherty, the All-Ireland Army Heavyweight champion – who is memorialised in bronze (photo: Irish Sporting Heritage).

Below: This statue, celebrating Irish-born Olympians Johnny Hayes, Matt McGrath and Bob Tisdall in Banba Square, Nenagh, is perhaps the finest sporting memorial in Ireland. Ger Ryan instigated the project to memorialise Nenagh's Olympians. The statue was part-funded by the National Roads Authority and unveiled by 1956 Olympic champion Ronnie Delaney in 2002 (photo: Damien Murphy).

VANISHED: BALDOYLE RACES, DUBLIN

Racing in the Baldoyle area began in 1829 at Deer Park, on a course laid out by racing enthusiast and landowner Thomas, Third Earl of Howth. By the 1830s, the races were held there over three days, and the local gentry flocked in great numbers to watch, gamble and socialise. The races ceased at Deer Park in 1842, but began again at Baldoyle in 1853. The site was perfect, as it was served by the Drogheda and Howth Railway Company, which regularly sponsored races.

The races at Baldoyle became hugely popular. They were cheap to attend and, as the racecourse was not enclosed, attracted all kind of hawkers, tricksters and pickpockets who could work the crowds. The unsavoury element was such that racing was stopped between 1861 and 1865, after a man was beaten to death in a fight. Such was the criminality attached to race days that the racecourse owners rebuilt the course to enclose it entirely, which allowed it to be policed more effectively, thereby keeping out the unwanted element. Stands, betting and show rings, as well as catering facilities were built, and updated into the early twentieth century, so that Baldoyle became the most modern and popular racecourse in Ireland.

Baldoyle remained a popular racecourse to attend, but the last addition to its facilities, a Tote office, was built in 1951. The other tracks that served Dublin – Leopardstown,

Baldoyle was by far the most popular racecourse in the early twentieth century, and the most up to date. This stand, which would be Baldoyle's main grandstand until its closure, was erected in 1919. It was built out of that most modern of materials, ferroconcrete and was the first of its kind in Ireland (picture: Irish Sporting Heritage).

After its closure, small pockets of land were successfully redeveloped, but the majority has remained derelict. Here the remains of the main stand are all that are left of what was once a pleasure ground for thousands of racegoers (photo: Damien Murphy).

Phoenix Park and the Curragh – upgraded their facilities more regularly, and by attracting a better class of horses and jockeys from the 1940s stole a march on Baldoyle.

When the racecourse insurers announced in 1968 that they would not guarantee the safety of the grandstand after 1973, the races at Baldoyle came to an end. The last meeting took place on 26 August 1972, and the key race days of Baldoyle were transferred to Leopardstown. After the demolition of the main grandstand in the mid-1980s, because its state of dereliction made it unsafe, the site was redeveloped, piece by piece, for housing. From the late 1990s and into the early 2000s, some 2,000 houses were built on the old racecourse, as well as a flood relief pumping station for the area. Since the economic downturn, the ongoing plans for the redevelopment of the site have stalled. Beyond the new houses lies a wasteland of open ground, as well as a few walls of racecourse buildings that have become a haven for graffiti artists. In none of the plans for the area, nor in the naming of the housing estates, has there been any attempt to commemorate what was once the lifeblood of Baldoyle.

During the Celtic Tiger years, the Baldoyle site was seen as ripe for redevelopment, including a major housing project called 'The Coast'. The development has fallen very far short of the original plan and the old racecourse remains, as it has been for years, a derelict wasteland (photo: Damien Murphy).

Rather than naming housing estates or the streets after famous racehorses, or parts of the old racecourse, there has been the construction of bland housing developments with the generic and placeless names of 'Castleross' and 'The Coast'. Given the sporting significance of the Baldoyle area, as a key component of the sporting heritage of Ireland and the bloodstock trade in particular, would it not have been better if at least one street had been named after Arkle who raced the course regularly, or Prince Regent, a legendary Baldoyle horse of the 1940s? Where once there were huge crowds, excitement and facilities that served the horse followers of the Dublin area, there is now dereliction, graffiti and a distant memory of nearly a century and a half of racing.

Baldoyle, like many other key Irish sporting sites, has vanished. Within a generation there will be few, if any, markers of the glamour days and the packed crowds it once attracted.

TEMPORARY: LAYTOWN RACES, MEATH

Horse racing is usually associated with lush, green grass and, when run as a commercial operation, features permanent stands, betting rings, restaurants and corporate boxes. Ireland is fortunate to play host to one of the few annual race meetings that does not conform to the standard contemporary model: the beach races at Laytown, County Meath. What started as a side attraction to the Boyne Regatta in 1868 has established itself as the only European beach race staged under the Rules of Racing. The original thinking was simply that a series of horse races, along the exposed beach at low tide, would amuse and occupy Regatta spectators while they waited for high tide and the continuation of the boating contests.

The beach races, however, eventually proved a greater draw than the Regatta and became a fixed feature in Irish seaside life in the late summer. Originally Laytown did not stand alone as a beach racing venue in the nineteenth and early twentieth centuries, as Miltown Malbay in Cork, Baltray in Louth and others also hosted summer race days.

Despite the history of beach racing, something that was once a common summertime event, it is Laytown that has stood the test of time, and perhaps this is due to its good social and political connections from its beginnings, and its transport links to the major cities of the island. Irish Parliamentary Party leader Charles Stewart Parnell acted as a steward for the beach races and, once the event secured

On race day, there are no fences or rails to guide the horses along the track, but rather a series of flags planted in the sand mark out the course (photo: Meath Tourism).

The attraction of Laytown Races, with easy rail access via the Dublin–Belfast line, has meant that crowds have flocked there across the decades on race day. Here, in the 1920s, a large crowd of happy day trippers is seen disembarking at the Laytown station, preparing themselves for a day at the seaside races (photo: National Library of Ireland).

the patronage of the local parish priest at the turn of the century, its future was secured. The races became a fixed event in the summer season calendar, were well organised, and attracted a large audience who travelled to Laytown by train from Dublin and Belfast on a branch line that had opened up the resort in 1844.

From 1909, those visitors who looked forward to the thrill of the beach races could also enjoy the Laytown and Bettystown Golf Club, which quickly established itself as one of the more impressive links courses on the east coast. The importance, for those who lived in seaside towns and for those who might visit, of attractions and facilities of a sporting nature are clear in the Laytown and Bettystown area. There was the annual spectacle of the beach races, the excellent links course, sea fishing and swimming. While the area never competed with seaside towns whose economy depended on tourism, such as Bray, the Laytown area developed a sporting infrastructure, including the beach races, which marked it out as a place that was, and remains, different and unique in sporting terms.

The races take place on the strand at low tide. Originally both five-furlong and two-mile races were run along the beach, but safety concerns now limit the races to a straight five-furlong dash along the beach. Crowds historically exceeded 10,000 people, but since the 1990s have settled at around 5,000. For the visitor today, the experience is essentially enjoyed in the same spirit as it was a century ago. Having arrived at the racecourse by train, car or coach, the spectator is aware that everything is temporary. The racecourse itself, the marquees and pavilions that provide food and drink, the toilets, the bookmakers and the tote, all are built each year for the races, and then taken down. Accompanying the 'official' aspect of the races are the hawkers and performers, all aware that the day out at Laytown offers them a chance to make some quick money.

Here, as the horses enter the final furlong of their race, and the finish line beckons, a lone figure can be seen on the seaward side of the photograph. At Laytown, as the course is straight and there is no inner course, spectators are allowed to stand only on the land side of the racecourse (photo: Meath Tourism).

Everything about Laytown is temporary, and all is placed in the sand only on the annual day of racing. Even the finishing line, shown here, is brought from storage and planted to mark where the race will finish that year. Once the tide turns, and the course covered by water, the races end for another year (photo: Irish Sporting Heritage).

Imagined: National Stadium, Dublin, and the Northern Ireland Stadium, Maze Prison site, Down

For all the stadia and sporting sites across the country that have actually been built, there have been many others which have been imagined but never realised. Two imagined sites of recent years are particularly significant, as they speak to larger themes in Irish society and the ways of modern sport.

In the late 1990s, as the economy of Ireland boomed, there was a belief amongst sports administrators and within government that new national stadia should be considered. The GAA was redeveloping Croke Park at the time, but long-term questions hung over the future of an ageing Lansdowne Road and also whether soccer, in the form of the FAI, should develop its own home and cease sharing Lansdowne with rugby. In 1998, Bertie Ahern announced a feasibility study, *A Stadium for a New Century*, which would assess whether a national stadium should be built, and if so, where it should be located and what sports and events it should cater for. The plan that emerged was for a major national stadium to be built in Abbotstown (designed by Behnisch Architekten) and, alongside it, a national sports campus which would promote and support a range of sports. The project was quickly linked with its main supporter, the Taoiseach of the time, and it was dubbed the 'Bertie Bowl'. In January 2000, the project was costed at £281 million, and by mid-2001 the projections had risen to £550 million, with fears that by the time of completion, the whole stadium complex would run up a bill of £1 billion. Given the rising costs, the sheer scale of the project (the stadium envisaged would have 80,000 seats) and fears that, despite inducements, the three main

sporting organisations might not take up residency, the plan for a national stadium was dropped in 2004. The decision was made instead to back the redevelopment of Lansdowne Road as a more cost-effective way of producing a state-of-the-art stadium for soccer and rugby. In the wake of the cancellation of the national stadium concept, the wider building of a sports campus at Abbotstown went ahead, and the site now encompasses the headquarters of the FAI, the Irish Institute of Sport and the Irish Sports Council, the National Aquatics Centre and the Morton Athletics Stadium.

An equally ambitious sporting stadium project was envisaged for the site of the former Long Kesh/Maze prison in Northern Ireland. The prison had housed the majority of paramilitary prisoners during the Northern Ireland conflict and was the stage of the 1981 hunger strikes, in which ten men died. Once the prison was closed in 2000, there was a degree of political uncertainty as to what to do with such a powerful site from the North's past. In 2006, it was announced that the majority of the site would be demolished (although certain prison buildings would be retained and protected), and in its place a national stadium built. This would have 42,500 seats, and be home to the GAA, IRFU and IFA in Northern Ireland. The plan for the site was drawn up the London company EDAW, who had conceived the master plan for the London 2012 Olympics, and the stadium was designed by HOK. Despite the sports bodies signing up to the plan, the spending of £140 million to redevelop a site of such contested memories was deeply problematic for parts of

The proposal to redevelop the site of the Long Kesh/Maze prison was the subject of intense political debate in the Northern Ireland Assembly. Despite the three main sporting bodies signing up to the idea, the plan was shelved, and money granted to redevelop Windsor Park, Casement Park and Ravenshill instead (photo: Irish Sporting Heritage).

the unionist community. In 2008, the First Minister Peter Robinson announced that the plan was dead. In 2011, it was announced that the money would be reallocated to the GAA (to redevelop Casement Park as a 40,000-seat venue), the IRFU (to upgrade Ravenhill) and the IFA (to rebuild Windsor Park). The former Maze prison site was also offered to the Royal Ulster Agricultural Society for staging their annual show.

The stories of the two imagined major stadia in Ireland of recent years reveal much. In the actual design and planning of the stadia, undertaken by leading firms in the field, there is little that can be faulted. The designs were,

at the time of their conception, state of the art. In Dublin the plans for the national stadium were seen as a personal vanity project by the then Taoiseach, and a scheme that would be prohibitively expensive when both the GAA and the IRFU already owned major stadia with large capacities in the capital. The plans for the former Maze site revealed the complexities of specific sites within the North, and the ways in which finding a new use for sites of conflict will often be difficult. In both plans, there were also real infrastructure issues: neither proposed site was connected to the rail system and road links were inadequate. Also, both stadia were on the outskirts of their respective cities, and lacked the necessary surroundings of restaurants, bars and hotels that sports followers expect for major fixtures. Major sport stadia, while necessary for international and national fixtures, are not (as has been shown by a succession of Olympic venues and stadia elsewhere in the world) a quick fix for the needs of the economy or issues of regeneration, they are not necessarily neutral sites that can obliterate the meanings associated with the past and they are not necessarily viable (or desirable) when a network of dated, but not defunct, stadia already exists.

Eircom Stadium was envisaged as the national stadium for Ireland, and was planned to be built in Abbotstown. Very similar in design to the Premier League grounds that were being built in England at the time, the plan was abandoned (photo: Irish Sporting Heritage).

TOURISM: K CLUB, COUNTY KILDARE

Hosting international sporting events, such as the Olympics or World Cup finals, is not only prestigious for the city or nation chosen to host, but also acts as an important revenue raiser and driver for tourism. While Ireland attracts travelling supporters on a regular basis for provincial and national rugby matches, and sporting tourists in golf, fishing and equestrian sports, the country is poorly placed to be able to compete in any bidding process for an event the size of the Olympics. In 2006, however, Ireland did host one of the largest sporting events in the calendar, and certainly the biggest in golf: the Ryder Cup.

In 1988, the Jefferson Smurfit Group purchased Straffan House and the surrounding farmland with a view to developing Ireland's premier golf destination. Arnold Palmer was hired to design a championship course and, in 1991, the course and a 36-bedroom hotel in the renovated Straffan House opened for business. A further eighteen-hole course, the Palmer Smurfit course, which was configured as an inland links course, followed. After reaching agreement with the PGA tour, the Smurfit European Open was staged on the original Palmer course from 1995 until 2003, and again in 2005. The close links between the club and the PGA, and Smurfit's long-term support for a major event on the European tour, were seen as vital when the decision was made as to which course should host the 2006 Ryder Cup.

In 2005, Smurfit and Michael Gannon purchased the club for an estimated €115 million, invested further money in the course, facilities and the hotel and built a series of luxury houses surrounding the course. In September 2006, the K Club hosted the Ryder Cup which, after an eventful tussle, was won by the Europeans. It is

Built in the Kildare countryside, the K Club is one of the premier golf destinations in Ireland (photo: The K Club).

estimated that total attendance at the course during practice and tournament was 130,000, and that nearly 2,000 media workers were also in attendance. In addition to the benefits to the Irish economy during the actual event (such as visitors, hotel bookings, sponsorship, exposure and so on), which averaged at a spend of €350 per day for each visitor, it was estimated by Deloitte that across the year the hosting of the event was directly worth €143 million to the economy as a whole. The Irish promotion of the event, its golf courses and the country as a whole, was seen as one of the most successful to date, and a 32 per cent increase on the revenues raised in 2002 when the event had been staged in Britain. When calculating what the tournament was worth in terms of the growth of Ireland as a golfing

Left: The course is built alongside the River Liffey, and many of the holes bring the water into play. In the distance lies Straffan House, now the centrepiece luxury hotel of the K Club (photo: The K Club).

Right: The K Club is best remembered for the 2006 Ryder Cup. Europe's victory was met with huge celebrations and also amongst the players. Here, two of Ireland's stars, Darren Clarke and Paul McGinley, begin their celebrations (photo: The K Club).

destination Deloitte estimated that this would amount to an income of some €240 million.

It is clear that the staging of such a high profile event is important. For three days in September 2006, the golfing and sporting eyes of the world were on County Kildare. The total global audience for the tournament was estimated at 6 million people and, for some of them, their exposure to the event, views of the K Club, the Liffey and the Irish countryside would have encouraged them to travel to Ireland for a golfing holiday. Certainly Fáilte Ireland saw the event as important to their strategy and anchored a tourist campaign around Ireland's golfing opportunities in its major markets. After the successful staging of the event, Fáilte Ireland concluded that 'the real value of the event is in its legacy to the country. The Ryder Cup was a fantastic platform to promote Ireland and Irish gold to a worldwide audience.'

Nevertheless, the model created by schemes such as the K Club, Ritz-Carlton and Mount Juliet, which combined golf resorts, apartments and hotel accommodation encouraged by generous tax breaks, was replicated across Ireland in a way that would prove to be eventually unsustainable. The flurry of building activity in the two years after the Ryder Cup meant that Ireland had more golf courses per capita than any other country in the world. Critics of these developments argued that they prized the economic bottom line above the impact on the natural landscape and properly planned housing developments.

In heritage terms, therefore, the legacy of the Ryder Cup is mixed. Nevertheless the K Club remains as one of the premier courses in the country, and the hotel accommodation, in the form of Straffan House built by the Barton family in the 1830s (and one of the best examples of French/Italian-inspired architecture in Ireland), is an architectural delight. It is the event that left an indelible mark. To play the course now is to walk in the footsteps of Tiger Woods, Padraig Harrington, Darren Clarke and others, and to bring back to life, at least in the mind, the great play, the tight matches, and the spectacular celebrations that followed. The K Club will, no matter how it might develop and change, forever be linked to all the successes of the 2006 Ryder Cup.

NAMING

The sense of history that surrounds sport, its athletes, feats and places is expressed in many forms. This book has been focused on the sites in which sport takes place, and how an understanding of heritage can be realised by examining them. One part of sport's heritage, which takes on no real physical form and yet is hugely important to our shared sense of the past, is in the use of naming buildings, bridges, stadia, fields, courses and even airports after sporting figures from history, or else in the manner in which non-sporting figures are celebrated in the naming of stadia.

Public buildings and structures all need names. In recent decades there have been a growing number of such civic spaces and places being named after Irish sporting heroes. In 2006, the decision was made, a few months after his death, to rename Belfast's City Airport, the George Best Belfast City Airport. It was a step that not only commemorated the city's most famous footballing son, but one that was applauded by all sections of Belfast's community. In 1987, eight years after he died, Cork's most talented hurler was honoured by Cork City Council in its decision to name a new city centre crossing of the River Lee after him, and the Christy Ring Bridge came into being. In the same city, the provincial GAA stadium, Páirc Uí Chaoimh, was named in honour of the long-serving Association General Secretary in 1976. Naming public sites and utilities is a key way of celebrating and remembering the sporting past.

The GAA, in particular, has used its stadia across the country as a way of paying tribute to a wide range of individuals from different backgrounds. In the 1890s, at the height of the Anglo- Boer War for example, many GAA clubs chose to show their support for the Boer cause, by renaming their clubs after Generals such as De Wet and

Pubs and hotels have, ever since the nineteenth century, provided refreshments and accommodation for sporting participants and spectators. Many of them, realising how important such sports-related business has been to their custom, have named their business after sporting types, personalities and locations. Here in Connemara, a hotel seeks to benefit from its association with angling tourists (Irish Sporting Heritage).

While there are a number of streets in Ireland that have been named to mark their proximity to sporting locations, there are very few towns and villages that take their names from a relationship with sport. In Tipperary, Horse and Jockey is one of the few exceptions (photo: Damien Murphy).

McAllister and McVeigh Park, home of Oisin GAA club in Glenariffe, County Antrim. The ground was named after two local men, Charlie McAllister and Pat McVeigh, who were killed by the British army on Tamlaght Bray in May 1924 (photo: Peter Higgins)

MacBride. Of the current GAA grounds across the country, around a third of them are named after political figures, a quarter after individuals who served the association, and around a tenth after saints or local Catholic clergy. While such historic naming is perhaps unproblematic in the Irish Republic, the naming of grounds, tournaments and trophies after paramilitaries from the period of the Northern conflict is considered problematic by many within the community. Ground naming such as the Kevin Lynch Club in Dungiven, County Derry, honouring the dead INLA hunger striker, or competition naming, such as the Mairead Farrell camogie championship in Tullysaran, County Armagh, commemorating the IRA member who was killed by the SAS in Gibraltar, link the GAA with a particular strand of Republicanism, and tie the games of the Association to politics with which some, especially in a post-conflict society, are uncomfortable.

At the more general level, sporting activity has given rise to the naming of places, such as Horse and Jockey in County Tipperary, and Hurler's Cross in County Clare.

Roads have frequently been named after local sporting sites, and examples across the country would include The Fairways and The Green in Bray, Tennis Court Lane in Skerries, Golf View in Listowel, Steeplechase Hill in Meath and Racecourse Hill in Clifden. In a similar vein, many commercial premises have named themselves after sports and sporting places, in an attempt to tie themselves to a sporting venue and attract more custom. Examples include the Hill 16 Pub in Dublin, the Fox and Hounds in Ballyvolane, County Cork, and the Pius's Polo Grounds (commemorating the Cavan victory in the 1947 All-Ireland final in New York) in Kilnaleck, County Cavan.

All these different levels of naming buildings and sites with sporting connotations is an important part of sporting heritage. The naming honours those who have passed before, the historic links between sport and place, and the centrality of sport within the civic community. Naming cements the links between places and sport, and in doing so prolongs the popular memory of traditions and myths that are central to the histories of any community.

Naming sports grounds after figures from Irish history is a dominant theme, particularly in the GAA, but has also been a feature of naming by local authorities. In Dublin, Eamonn Ceannt Park, a local athletics track, is named to honour the executed signatory to the 1916 Proclamation (photo: Dublin City Libraries).

CONCLUSION

Iʀᴇʟᴀɴᴅ's sᴘᴏʀᴛɪɴɢ ʜᴇʀɪᴛᴀɢᴇ is, as this book has attempted to show, rich and varied. It encompasses sporting places as varied as links golf courses, which have worked with a landscape shaped by the sea and stadia constructed using the latest technology. Often sporting places, as with road bowling and beach racing, are occasional events, which use natural and manmade contours and pathways to allow people to play. Many sports, especially those built around private clubs, have developed, for over a century and more, with tidy clubhouses, courts and pitches, which allow their members to play in sociable comfort, in a manner their Victorian forebears would recognise. There are also major stadia designed to cater for crowds in their thousands on a regular basis, racing routes designed for the noise and power of the internal combustion petrol engine, and places where once people played, but all now has gone silent.

All these places, from the humble local handball alley to the opulence of the Trinity College cricket pavilion, from the urban concrete of Windsor Park through to the grandeur and exclusivity of Fitzwilliam Tennis Club, have to be considered as part of Ireland's heritage. These are the spaces and places where the Irish people of all classes have, since the middle of the nineteenth century, come to play. In the hours between work and sleep, and on the key weekend days, whether as spectators or competitors, people across Ireland have gathered in sporting sites to exercise, socialise and to build communities. Most of this heritage is not, in the strict aesthetic or architectural sense, worth much notice. These are predominantly utilitarian structures or spaces. They are clubhouses, changing rooms, terraces, stadiums and places where the workers – greenkeepers, professionals and administrators – are housed. The central issue here is not one of architectural

Not all sporting spaces are products of clubs and associations. Many are open spaces that are spontaneously used for play. Here, in 1978, youngsters in Fatima Mansions play an improvised version of cricket, with a camán replacing the usual bat (photo: Dublin City Libraries).

value, but one of social history. Sport has been a constant in the lives of the Irish, when many other aspects of daily life have been changed by technology or fallen out of fashion. These sporting sites are the venues of a shared social memory. They may, at the elite level, be the place where the great game was won, the wonder try scored or the record broken. At the popular pastime and local level, they are the places where people relaxed and socialised, where friendly rivalries were joined, and the spaces where children learned to play and became the next generation of custodians of the local sporting myths and legends.

The importance of sporting sites is multifaceted. They are part of the tourist economy. They provide employment, and support many businesses who set up around them. They bring top athletes from around the world to compete in Ireland and, in doing so, turn the gaze of the world on the country. They have helped form and have cemented various identities around religion, gender, class and nation. In the context of education and workplace, they have been part of the sporting revolution and have formed institutional identities. And for all these sites, no matter how poor or rich, they have left a footprint in terms of buildings, courses, pitches, tracks, stands, fields and terraces. None of them will last forever, but their presence in the landscape signals and records how important sport is to the economy, to the well-being of the population's health, to issues of inclusion and exclusion, to the heroic feat of yesterday and the sports star of tomorrow. As Ireland, like the rest of the world, changes and develops, let us remember that we all, in our busy lives, need a place to play and, when we do so, let us recognise that the places in which we play speak to the lives of the generations who went before us, and will speak to those who come after we have gone.

Above: Much of Ireland's sporting environment has been the product of people's voluntary efforts, their hard work and their desire to provide their community with a place to play. Here in An Cheathrú Rua, a club founded in 1967, and only the second Connemara team ever to win the Galway Senior football title (in 1996), a hand-painted sign announces that the grounds are closed (photo: Irish Sporting Heritage).

Pearse Square, Dublin, in the 1970s, and home to a game of soccer for a group of young boys. The site has now changed, but for a brief while the open space provided a sporting site for urban youngsters who otherwise may not have had access to sports facilities (photo: Dublin City Libraries).

Match-day signs announce the admission prices at Waterfoot GAA Club, County Antrim (photo: Peter Higgins).

SELECT BIBLIOGRAPHY

Bale, John, *Sport and Place: A Geography of Sport in England, Scotland and Wales* (London: E and FN Spon, 1982).

Bale, John, 'The place of "place" in cultural studies in sports' in *Progress in Human Geography* 1998, 12 (4): 507-524.

Brodie, Malcolm (ed.), *Irish Football League 1890–1990: Official Centenary History* (Belfast: Irish Football League Ltd, 1990)

Carey, Tim, *Croke Park: A History* (Cork: The Collins Press, 2007).

Comerford, Vincent, *Ireland Inventing the Nation* (London: Arnold, 2003)

Costello, Con, *A Most Delightful Station: the British Army on the Curragh of Kildare, Ireland, 1855–1922* (Cork: The Collins Press, 1996).

Cronin, Mike, *Sport and Nationalism in Ireland: Gaelic Games, Soccer and Irish Identity Since 1884* (Dublin: Four Courts Press, 1999).

Cronin, Mike, Mark Duncan and Paul Rouse, *The GAA: A People's History* (Cork: The Collins Press, 2009).

Curtis, L. Perry, 'Stopping the Hunt', in Charles H. E. Philbin (ed.), *Nationalism and Popular Protest in Ireland* (Cambridge: Cambridge University Press, 1987)

Daly, Tom, *The Rás: the Story of Ireland's Unique Bike Race* (Cork: The Collins Press, 2003)

D'Arcy, Fergus, *Horses, Lords and Racing Men: the Turf Club, 1790–1990* (Kildare: The Turf Club, 1991)

Davison, Stephen, *Hard Roads* (Belfast: Blackstaff, 2008)

Dease Edmund, F., *A Complete History of the Westmeath Hunt from its Foundation* (Dublin: Browne and Nolan, 1898)

Dooley, Terence, *The Decline of the Big House in Ireland: A Study of Irish Landed Families 1860–1960* (Dublin: Wolfhound Press, 2001)

Farmer, Tony, *Privileged Lives: A Social History of the Irish Middle Classes, 1882–1989* (Dublin: Farmer, 2009).

Garnham, Neal, *Association Football and Society in Pre-partition Ireland* (Belfast: Ulster Historical Foundation, 2004)

Glynn, Enda, *A Century of Golf at Lahinch, 1892–1922* (Lahinch: Lahinch Golf Club, 1991)

Hanna, Wilfred J. (ed.), *A Farewell to Ormeau: North of Ireland Cricket Ground* (Belfast: North of Ireland Cricket Club, 2001)

Havelin, Harry (assisted by Sean Bissett and Richard Agnew), *A History of Motor Cycle Sport in Ireland, 1902–2002* (Dublin: Motor Cycle Union of Ireland, 2002)

Holt, Richard, *Sport and the British* (Oxford: Oxford University Press, 1989).

Horner, Arnold, 'Dublin's expanding golfscape' in *Irish Geography*, 1993, 26 (2): 151-15

Hunt, Tom, *Sport and Society in Victorian Ireland: the Case of Westmeath* (Cork: Cork University Press, 2007)

Inglis, Simon, *Played in Manchester. The architectural heritage of a city at play* (London: English Heritage, 2004).

Lane, Fintan, *Long Bullets: A History of Road Bowling in Ireland* (Ardfield: Galley Head Press, 2005)

Lewis, Colin A., *Hunting in Ireland: An Historical and Geographical Analysis* (London: J. A. Allen and Company, 1975)

McAnallen, Donal, David Hassan and Roddy Hegarty, (eds.) *The Evolution of the GAA, Pobal, Club, Contae agus Tir* (Belfast: Ulster Historical Foundation, 2009).

McCook, Alastair, *The Power and the Glory: the History of the North West 200* (Belfast: Appletree, 2002)

Martin, John, *Tales of the Dogs: a Celebration of the Irish and their Greyhounds* (Belfast: Blackstaff, 2009)

Meenan, James and Clarke, Desmond (eds.), *RDS the Royal Dublin Society, 1731–1981* (Dublin: Gill & Macmillan, 1981)

Menton, William A., *The Golfing Union of Ireland, 1891–1991* (Dublin: Gill & Macmillan, 1992)

Montgomery, Bob, *The Irish Gordon Bennett Race 1903*, (Meath: Dreoilín, 1999)

Murphy, Colm, *Long Shadows by De Banks: a History of the Blue, Yellow and Green* (Cork: Cork County Cricket Club, 2005)

Murphy, Derek, 'Par for the Course', *Plan: the Art of Architecture and Design*, November 2008, pp 65–7.

Nolan, Brendan, *Phoenix Park: A History and Guidebook* (Dublin: The Liffey Press, 2006).

O'Brien, Gearoid, *Belvedere House Gardens and Park: The Official Guide* (Mullingar: Belvedere, 2000)

O'Brien, Thomas (ed.), *Carlow County Football Club Rugby History, 1873–1977* (Carlow: Nationalist and Leinster Times, 1977)

Priestley, Ciarán, *The Enduring Legacy of an Idle Youth* (Dublin: Ciarán Priestley, 2010)

Reid, Tony, *Bohemian AFC, Official Club History 1890–1976* (Dublin: Tara Publishing Company Ltd for Bohemian Association Football Club, 1977)

Siggins, Gerard, *Green Days: Cricket in Ireland, 1792–2005* (Stroud: Nonsuch Publishing Ltd, 2005)

Siggins, Gerard and Clerkin, Malachy, *Lansdowne Road: the Stadium, the Matches, the Greatest Days* (Dublin: O'Brien Press, 2010)

Swan, Desmond A., *History of the Curragh of Kildare: 50th Anniversary of Defence Forces Week* (Curragh Camp: An Cosantóir, 1972).

Tranter, Neil, *Sport, Economy and Society in Britain, 1750–1914* (Cambridge: Cambridge University Press, 1998)

West, Trevor, *The Bold Collegians: The Development of Sport in Trinity College, Dublin* (Dublin: Lilliput Press, 1991)

Abbotstown, County Dublin 246, 248
Aer Lingus 51, 66, 226–227
Aer Lingus Social and Athletic Association (ALSAA) 226–227
Aga Khan Challenge 123
Aghavannagh Barracks, Wicklow 214, 216
Ahern, Bertie 246
Aiken, Frank 109, 114
Alexandra, Queen 141
All-Ireland Polo Club 230, 231
Amateur Athletics Association 19
An Cheathrú Rua, Connemara 255
Annaverna Mountain, County Louth 76
Ardscull, County Kildare 190
Armagh, County, road bowling in 182–185
Arsenal 20
Ashtown, Dublin 115
Aviva Stadium 1, 5, 7, 81, 89–92, 117
Avondale House, County Wicklow 213–216

Baldoyle Racecourse, Dublin 80, 89, 143, 145, 176, 238–240
Ballybunnion Golf Course, County Kerry 6, 71
Ballymena Bowling Club, County Antrim 36
Ballymoney, County Antrim 236
Ballynahinch Castle, County Galway 196–199
Bandon, County Cork 185
Barry, Michael 6
Barton, Amanda 212
Beamish, Richard 141
Belfast Celtic 42
Belfast City Airport 251
Belle Vue, Manchester 116, 117
Bellewstown Racecourse, County Meath 70
Belvedere Hunting Lodge, County Westmeath 169–172
Belvedere Rugby Football Club 103
Bennett, James Gordon 191
Berney, Jim 50
Berridge, Richard 197
'Bertie Bowl' 246
Best, George 128, 251
Blackrock Baths, Dublin 166, 167–168
Bohemian Football Club 93, 103, 105, 230
Ból Chumann na hÉireann 185
Bolton Wanderers 20
Bord na gCon (Irish Greyhound Board) 118, 158
Bowling League of Ireland 163
Bradford 20, 77
Bray Athletic Ground 72
Bray, County Wicklow 49, 253
Bray Unknowns 72
Bray Wanderers 72
Breffni Park, Cavan 25
Browning, F. H. 90
Bruen, Henry 142
Burke, John 150

Butler, James 232
Butterly, Maurice 93
Buttevant Castle, County Cork 40
Byrne, Tony 234

Carlisle Grounds, Bray 72
Carlow Football Club, Oak Park 142–145
Carlow Golf Club 142, 144
Carlow Mental Hospital 64
Carlton, Christopher 175
Carnalea Golf Club, Bangor, County Down 73
Carrickmore GAA club, County Tyrone 84
Casement Park, Belfast 133–138
Casement, Roger 138
Castle, Richard 172
Catholic Young Men's Society (CYMS) 59
Celtic Park, Belfast 117
Central Council for Physical Recreation 27
Chapel Allerton, Leeds 21
Christle, Joe 205
Christy Ring Bridge, Cork 251
City and Suburban Racecourse, Jones Road, Dublin 93
City of Derry Motorcycle Club 209
Civil Service Cricket Club 66, 230
Clarke, Darren 250
Clarke, Jim 117
Cliftonville Soccer Club, Belfast 29, 124
Clongowes Wood College, County Kildare 60
Clonliffe Harriers, Dublin 200
Cochrane, Sir Stanley Herbert 228, 229
Coláiste Einde, Galway, handball courts 146–148
Coleraine and District Motor Club 209
Collins, Jerry 117
Colthurst, Sir George C. 140
Commercial Club 180
Community Games 65
Cooney, John C. 209
Cooper, George 109, 110
Corbett, 'Gentleman Jim' 114
Cork and County Cricket Club 140
Cork Constitution 65
Cork County Cricket Club, The Mardyke, Cork 139–141
Cork, County, road bowling in 182–185
Corrigan Park, Belfast 133
Costigan, Daniel 180
Coughlan, Eamonn 200
County Dublin Polo Club 230
Craigavad House, County Down 73
Croke Park, Dublin 9, 77, 81, 84, 87, 93–96, 246
    Hill 16 93, 95, 96
    Hogan Stand 95, 96
Cross, Dorothy 148
Crossmaglen Rangers 40, 87
Curragh, the, County Kildare 52, 97–102, 110, 239

Curraghmore 19
Curraghmore Hunt 172
Curran, Captain Richard 12
Cusack, Michael 51, 54, 200
Cusack Park, Ennis 129
Cushendall, County Antrim 75
Czostak, Anton 114

D'Alton, Cardinal 138
Dalymount Park, Dublin 90, 103–105
Dargan, William 72
de Caters, Baron Pierre 191
Defence Forces 62
Defence Forces Athletic Association 66
Delaney, Ronnie 237
Derry City (Soccer Club) 42
Dineen, Frank 96
Diveney, Danny 137
Dizengremel, Laury 234
Donabate, County Dublin 55
Donnelly, Dan 50, 109, 110
Donore Harriers, Dublin 200–201
Dough Castle, Lahinch, County Clare 154
Dowdall, Paddy 114
Down Royal Corporation of Horsebreeders 173
Down Royal Racecourse, County Down 42, 173–179
Doyle, Jack 83, 236
Dr Cullen Park, Carlow 129
Drew, Thomas 222, 223
Drogheda and Howth Railway Company 238
Dublin Camogie County Board 232
Dublin Eagles 116
Dublin Lawn Tennis Club 159
Dublin Metropolitan Police 180
Dublin University Boat Club 180
Dublin University Central Athletic Club 223
Dun Laoghaire Baths 164, 165, 168
Duncannon Races, County Wexford 23
Dundalk, County Louth 57
Dundalk Football Club, County Louth 49
Dundalk GNR 49
Dundalk Young Irelands GAA club 73
Dunlop, Henry William 89
Dunlop, Joey 212, 236
Duque, Orlando 28

Eamonn Ceannt Park, Dublin 253
Eason, Charles 162
Edgbaston, Birmingham 21
Edgeworth, Maria 197
Edward VII, King 141
Eircom Stadium 248
Elizabeth II, Queen 96

Emigration museum, Cobh 15
Emirates Stadium 20
Europa Cup 51

FAI Cup 66, 115
FAI (Football Association of Ireland) 5, 90, 92, 105, 246
Fallon, Gerry 76
Farrelly, Dermot J. 180
Fatima Mansions, Dublin 254
Fethard Hunt, County Tipperary 10
Fitzgerald, Desmond 227
Fitzgerald, Dick 129
Fitzgerald Stadium, Killarney 129–132
Fitzgibbon Cup 61
Fitzwilliam Tennis Club, Dublin 159–161
Flaherty, Mike 236
Flannery, Con 181
Foot Races Committee 221
Football Association 19
Football Association of Ireland (FAI) 5, 90, 92, 105, 246
Forty Foot, Dalkey, County Dublin 42
Fraher, Dan 12
Fraher Field, Dungarvan, County Waterford 12, 75

Gaelic Athletic Association (GAA) 19, 38, 39, 40, 42, 44, 51, 54, 55, 58,
   77, 93, 129, 155, 158, 216, 246, 247, 251
Gaelic Field, Shandon, Dungarvan, County Waterford 12
Gaelic Grounds, Limerick 158
Galway Racecourse 26
Gannon, Michael 249
Garda Rowing Club, Dublin 180–181
Garryowen Club, Limerick 158
George Best Belfast City Airport 251
George II, King 175
George IV, King 98
Glasgow Celtic 105
Glasgow Rangers 124
Glenmalure Park, Milltown, Dublin 86
Gogarty, Oliver St John 223
Goggins, Rodney 59
Golf Hotel, Lahinch, County Clare 152
Golfing Union of Ireland 149
Gordon Bennett Motor Race 190–192
Grace, W. G. 87, 141
Grand Prix 68, 232
Great Southern and Western Railway (GSWR) 8, 102, 150
Green, Ronnie 116
Greene, Philip 55
Greville, Lord 62
Guinness 66, 200, 226
Guinness Athletic Union (GAU) 66
Guinness, Edward 1, 2, 63
Guinness, Rupert Edward Cecil Lee 1

Hackett, Eddie 80
Hall, Tom 50
Handball Courts, Coláiste Einde, Galway 146–148
Harold, G. W. 142
Harold's Cross, Dublin 115
Hassetts Cross, Limerick 158
Hayes Hotel, Thurles, County Tipperary 54
Hayes, Johnny 237
Heritage Ireland 9, 11
Heysel, Brussels 20
Highbury 20, 21
Hill, Arthur 173, 175, 217
Hill, Damon 232
Hillsborough, 77 20
Hogan, Michael 96
Horse and Jockey, County Tipperary 251, 253
Horse Show, Dublin 119, 120, 121, 123, 230
Horseshoe Pitchers Association 30
Howard-Bury, Colonel Charles Kenneth 172
Hurler's Cross, County Clare 253
Hydro, Tramore, County Waterford 85

IFA (Irish Football Association) 19, 90, 93, 105, 124, 126, 127, 246, 247
Ingle, Jimmy 114
Inis Mór 28
Inishcrone Cliff Baths, County Sligo 11
International Motor Race 68, 190, 232
IRFU (Irish Rugby Football Union) 19, 89, 90, 92, 158, 246, 247
Irish Amateur Athletics Association (IAAA) 58, 200
Irish Amateur Boxing Association (IABA) 109, 112, 114
Irish Amateur Rowing Union 180
Irish Bowling Association 163
Irish Champion Athletics Club (ICAC) 89, 200
Irish Cycling Association 155
Irish Derby 51, 97, 117, 158
Irish Football Association (IFA) 19, 90, 93, 105, 124, 126, 127, 246, 247
Irish Greyhound Board (Bord na gCon) 118, 158
Irish Greyhound Derby 115, 118
Irish Handball Alley Project 147
Irish Heritage Trust 9–11
Irish International Motor Race 68
Irish Railway Company 49
Irish Rugby Football Union (IRFU) 19, 89, 90, 92, 158, 246, 247
Irish Rugby Union Volunteer Corps (IRUVC) 90
Irish Senior Hockey Cup 193
Irish Turf Club 54
Irish Women United 161
Island Golf Club, Donabate, County Dublin 55
Islandbridge, Dublin 180, 181
Iveagh Trust 63
Iveagh Trust Public Baths, Dublin 63, 167

Jefferson Smurfit Group 249
Joyce, James 60

K Club, County Kildare 249–250
Keady, County Armagh 185
Kelly, David 92
Kevin Lynch Club, Dungiven, County Derry 253
Kilkenny Castle 66
Kilmainham Gaol 81
Kingstown Boat Club 188
Kingstown Royal Harbour Boat Club 188
Kinnegar, Holywood, County Down 73

Lahinch, County Clare 57
Lahinch Golf Club, County Clare 149–154
Lansdowne Road Stadium 1, 5, 77, 80, 81, 87, 89, 90, 91, 92, 96, 103, 246
Laytown and Bettystown Golf Club, County Meath 244
Laytown Races, County Meath 241–245
Leinster 100 (Road Race) 209
Leinster Rugby 123
Leinster Schools Cup 33, 61
Leinster Schools Junior Cup 217
Leinster Senior Cup 103
Leitch, Archibald 20, 21, 105, 124
Leopardstown Racecourse, Dublin 77, 238, 239
Levinge, Sir Richard 172
Liffey Swim 166
Limerick AFC 158
Limerick Races 43
Linfield Football Club 124, 126
Listowel and Ballybunnion Lartigue Railway 6
Liverpool 20
Long Kesh/Maze prison, County Down 246, 247

McAlery, John 29
McAlinden, Hugh 117
McAlinden, Patsy 117
McAllister and McVeigh Park, Glenariffe, County Antrim 252
McAllister, Charlie 252
McCormack, John 228
McGinley, Paul 250
McGrath, Matt 237
MacKenzie, Alister 152
McKillop, Father George 75
McManus, J. P. 158
McRandall, Danny 138
McVeigh, Pat 252
Magilligan Strand, County Derry 210
Maher, Joey 234
Maide Ban, County Cavan 83
Mairead Farrell camogie championship 253
Manchester United 20, 81
Mannion, Sean 236

Markets Field, Limerick 155–158
Martin, Richard 197
Martin, Richard (Humanity Dick) 197
Mehigan, Paddy 55
Melba, Nellie 228
Merckx, Eddie 208
Morgan, Gerry 124
Morris, Old Tom 152
Morrison, Billy 167
Motor Cycle Union of Ireland (MCUI) 209
Mount Murray, Bunbrosna, County Westmeath 62
Mourne Grange School, Kilkeel, County Down 35
Mullingar Cricket Club 62
Mullingar Golf Club 169
Mulvany, John Skipton 188
Murphy, David 182
Murphy, Pat 202
Murphy, W. R. E. 114
Museum of Country Life, Mayo 11

Na Piarsaigh Stadium, Rosmuc, County Galway 30
Na Shuler XL 106, 141
National Athletics and Cycling Association 58
National Boxing Stadium, Dublin 109–114
National Cycling Association (NCA) 202, 207
National Heritage Council 9
National Inventory of Architectural Heritage 11, 218
National Lottery 9, 58
National Museum 11
National Stadium 246, 248
Navan Cycling and Athletic Grounds 209
Nenagh, County Tipperary 237
Neptune Club 180, 181
Newbrook Racecourse, Mullingar, County Westmeath 62
Newcastle United 81
North of Ireland, Cricket Club, Ormeau, Belfast 106–108
North of Ireland Football Club 107
North West 200, Antrim and Derry 209–212
Northern Cricket Union 108
Northern Ireland Stadium 246–248

Ó Colmáin, Gearóid 114
Oak Park, Carlow 142–145
Obermauer, Niiki 114
O'Caoimh, Padraig 58
O'Connell, Daniel 97, 197
O'Connor Jnr, Christy 228
O'Donoghue, Paddy 117
O'Dwyer, Declan 227
O'Dwyer, Michael 66
O'Hehir, Micheál 55
Oisin GAA club, Glenariffe, County Antrim 252
Old Trafford 81

Old Wesley rugby club 61
Omagh Tennis Club 77
O'Malley, Grace 197
O'Rourke, Michael 59
O'Sullivan, Dr Eamonn 131

Pairc Colmcille, Carrickmore GAA club, County Tyrone 84
Pairc Eire Óg, County Louth 73
Páirc Uí Chaoimh, Cork 251
Pallas Green, County Limerick 234, 235
Palmer, Arnold 249
Papworth, George 189
Parnell, Charles Stewart 106, 214, 215, 216, 241
Parnell, Hayes 216
Parnell, John Henry 214, 216
Pearse Square, Dublin 67, 255
Pembroke Wanderers Hockey Club, Dublin 193–195
Pentland, John 217, 218
Pettit, Tom 1
Phoenix Cricket Club 214, 216, 230, 233
Phoenix Park, Dublin 68, 230–233
    Fifteen Acres 230, 232
    Nine Acres 230
Phoenix Park Racecourse 230
Pisser Dignam's Field, Phibsborough, Dublin 103
Poc Fada championship 76
Polo Club, All-Ireland 230, 231
Populous (architects) 92
Portland, John 217
Portmarnock Golf Club 42
Portstewart, County Derry 13
Prior, Jim 124
Punchestown Races, Naas, County Kildare 172

Railway and Steampacket Company Irish Athletic and Social Union 162
Railway Union Bowls Club, Dublin 162–163
Railway Union Sports Club 66
Rainbow Rapids, Dun Laoghaire 168
Ranjitsinhji, Prince (Ranji) 197, 198, 199
Rás Tailteann 202–208, 230
Rathdrum Rugby Club 215
Real Tennis Court, Dublin 1, 2, 3, 7
Reardon, Jimmy 200
Red Bull Steeple Cross 40
Redmond, John 214
Rennie, John 188
Ring, Christy 138
Robinson, Peter 247
Roche, Jem 59
Roche, Stephen 208
Rochfort, Robert 172
Roddy, Joe 57
Rosmuc, County Galway 30, 236

Rossenarra Stud Farm, Kilkenny 87
Rosses Point Golf Club, County Sligo 11
Rowing Association 19
Royal Belfast Golf Club 73
Royal Dublin Golf Club 230
Royal Dublin Society (RDS) Showgrounds, Dublin 119–123
Royal Hospital Donnybrook 61
Royal Irish Yacht Club 188
Royal St George Yacht Club, Dun Laoghaire 186–189
Royal Victorian Baths, Dun Laoghaire 164, 168
Royal Whip 98
Rudge Whitworth cycle manufacturers 37
Rugby 23
Rugby Football Union 19
Rushbrooke Lawn Tennis and Croquet Club, Cobh, County Cork 73
Rustlings, Sheffield 21
Ryan, Carmel 185
Ryan, Ger 237
Ryan, Patrick/Paddy 234, 235
Ryder Cup 51, 249, 250

St Anne's Golf Club, Dublin 24, 73–75
St Dympna's Hospital, Carlow 131
St Finian's Mental Hospital, Killarney 131
St James Park 81
St James's Gate Football Club 66
St Kevin's GAA club, Bray 72
St Mary's Field, Dublin 115
St Patrick's College, Maynooth, swimming pool 62
Semple Stadium, County Tipperary 78
Shamrock Rovers 86, 123
Shannon Rowing Clubhouse, Limerick 16
Shaw, Joe 117
Shelbourne Football Club 39, 115
Shelbourne Park, Dublin 115–118
Shelbourne Tigers 116
Sigerson, George 16
Skibbereen, County Cork 182
Sligo, County 11
Smith, William Clifford 16
Smyth, Edward 119
South of Ireland Golf Championship 152
Special Olympics 51
Spencer, Earl 89, 96
Straffan House 249
Sullivan, John 114
Sunday's Well Tennis Club 141

Tait, Sir Peter 16
Templemore Public Baths, Belfast 167
Thomond Park, Limerick 77, 79, 158
Tisdall, Bob 237
Tolka Park, Dublin 39

Tramore Races, County Waterford 174
Tranter, Neil 17
Treacy, John 201
Trinity College, Dublin 61, 123, 141, 162, 180, 220–225
    College Park 87, 200, 220, 221, 223
Trinity Pavilion 222
Tullysaran, County Armagh 253
Turf Club, Kildare 97

Ulster Grand Prix 209, 212
University Athletic Club 221
University College, Dublin 1, 123

Villeneuve, Jacques 232
Volvo Ocean Race 82

Waterfoot GAA Club, County Antrim 256
Waterford Hunt 170
Waterhouse, Samuel 200
Watson, Tom 228
Wesley College, Dublin 61
West Clare Railway 149, 150
Western Railway 49
Westmeath Hunt 170, 172
Westmeath Hunt Club 172
Wexford Bull Ring 33
Wicklow County Cricket Club 215
William III, King 175
Wilson, Andrew 217
Wilson, Wesley William 2
Wilson's Hospital, Westmeath 217–219
Wimbledon Dons 116
Winchester 23
Windsor Park, Belfast 105, 124–128
Wingfield, Major Walter 21
Wood, Sanction 102
Woodbrook Cricket Club, Wicklow 228
Woodbrook Golf Club, Wicklow 228–229
Woodenbridge Golf Club, Wicklow 45
Wyatt, James 215